*Jabberwoke Pocket Occult Collection*

~

*Crystal Gazing* by Frater Achad

*Heavenly Bridegrooms* by Ida Craddock

*Moonchild* by Aleister Crowley

*The Kybalion* by Three Initiates

*The So-Called Occult* by Carl Jung

*The Great God Pan* by Arthur Machen

*The Witch Cult* by Margaret Murray

*The Book of Lies* by Frater Perdurabo

*A Midsommar Night's Dream* by William Shakespeare

*Satan: A Novel* by Mark Twain

~

# HEAVENLY BRIDEGROOMS

## Ida Craddock

Introduction / Afterwards by
Aleister Crowley & Theodore Schroeder, Esq.

JABBERWOKE
San Francisco

HeavenlyBridegrooms.com

# HEAVENLY BRIDEGROOMS

HEAVENLY BRIDEGROOMS, reprinted in
the medical journal *Alienist and Neurologist*, has
been left entirely unedited by Mr. Theodore
Schroeder, with the exception of a brief explan-
atory note. I must say that it is one of the most
remarkable human documents ever produced,
and it should certainly find a regular publisher
in book form. The authoress of the MS. claims
that she was the wife of an Angel. She expounds
at the greatest length the philosophy connected
with this thesis. Her learning is enormous. She
finds traces of similar beliefs in every country in
the world, and (having a similar experience of
her own) she can hardly be blamed for arguing
that one thing confirms the other. Mr.
Schroeder is quite logical in calling her paper
*'An Unintentional Contribution to the Erotogenetic
Interpretation of Religion,'* but commits the errors
of *petitio principii* and *non distributio medii* with the
most exquisite nonchalance. Only a lawyer
could be so shameless. He begs the question
with regard to this particular case, assuming
that her relation with the angel was pure
hallucination, of which he has no evidence
whatsoever. He argues that, since one person
both loves and is religious, religion is nothing
but a morbid manifestation of the sexual instinct. One does not have even to disagree with

him to see how worthless is his reasoning. As a matter of fact, I do half agree with him in my calmer moments in a general way, but the conclusion can be carried a step further. When you have proved that God is merely a name for the sex instinct, it appears to me not far to the perception that the sex instinct is God.

This particular MS. is sane in every line. The fact that the woman committed suicide twelve or fifteen years afterwards is no more against the sanity of the MS. than the suicide of Socrates proves that the *Republic* is merely the lucubration of a lunatic. I am very far from agreeing with all that this most talented woman sets forth in her paper, but she certainly obtained initiated knowledge of extraordinary depth. She seems to have had access to certain most concealed sanctuaries. I should personally be inclined to attribute her suicide rather to the vengeance of the guardians of those palaces than to any more obvious cause. She has put down statements in plain English which are positively staggering. This book is of incalculable value to every student of occult matters. No Magick library is complete without it.

*Baphomet*

ALEISTER CROWLEY.

*A selection from*
## ALIENIST AND NEUROLOGIST
### SPRING 1916, VOLUME XXXVII

## An Explanatory Note
### by Theodore Schroder

IN THE COURSE OF my studies on the eroto-
genesis of religion, I became interested in the life
work and mental characteristics of one Ida C., a
woman who committed suicide in her fourty-
fifth year. I first heard of her after her death, but
it seemed to me that a psychologic study of her
would yield rich materials as a contribution to
the psychology of religion. Consequently, I
bestirred myself to secure information, both
biographical and auto-biographical. Amoung
the materials gathered was her life long correspondence with friends, a number of published
essays written by her, some scraps of manuscripts, and two completed but unpublished
book manuscripts. Ida. C. was for a number of
years a college teacher and for a long time
associated with various kinds of free-thinking
heretics. She was never married. In due time she
became the victim of erotic hallucinations to
which she gave a "spiritual" interpretation. Later, when her conduct brought her to the verge
of incarceration in a jail or in an asylum, she
endeavored frankly to meet the issue of her own
insanity. The resultant investigation to her mind
seemed a complete vindication, not only of her

sanity, but also, of the objective reality and spirituality of her erotic experiences. This vindication she reduced to writing. This manuscript is now in my possession. It seems to me under the circumstances of the case that this is too valuable a document to be mutilated by editing. Furthermore, others should be given equal opportunity with myself in the interpretation of this material. The manuscript has been revised by its author and in a number of places it was quite impossible to decipher the interlineations, or replace words destroyed by the tearing of the manuscript through frequent handling before it came into my possession. At such places a word may be occasionally omitted or a connection left defective, otherwise the following document is the exact words of its author. This essay, I believe, was written before her thirty-fifth year, ten years before her suicide. Just before she wrote this she was a short time a voluntary inmate of an asylum and pronounced incurably insane. She left the country to escape legal confinement.

THEODORE SCHROEDER, ESQ.

# HEAVENLY BRIDEGROOMS

*An Unintentional Contribution to the*
*Erotogenetic Interpretation of Religion*

By Ida C.—

*And it came to pass; when man began to multiply upon the earth, the Sons of God saw that the daughters of men were fair, and they took of them wives of all that they chose.*

*— Genesis 6:2*

## Preface

IT HAS been my high privilege to have some practical experience as the earthly wife of an angel from the unseen world. In the interests of psychical research, I have tried to explore this pathway of communication with the spiritual universe, and, so far as lay in my power, to make a sort of rough guidebook of the route. For not all wives of HEAVENLY BRIDEGROOMS travel the same path at first. There are roads running into this one from every religion and folklore under the sun, since the pathway of marital relations on the Borderland was once, and still is, as I hope to show, one of the main thoroughfares connecting our world with the world beyond the grave. This thoroughfare, along part of which I hope to conduct the reader in imagination, is marked with signposts, many crumbling under the religious storms of centuries, others preserved as sacred trellises upon which to train a rank growth of flourishing superstition, and still others fresh with modern paint and gilding. Part of this thoroughfare runs straight through the Christian Church, or, to speak more accurately, the foundations of the Church are laid upon this very principle. For Jesus himself is said to be the child of a union between an earthly woman and a HEAVENLY

BRIDEGROOM who (however godlike, and whatever the details of the relation) certainly seems to have manifested to Mary on the occult plane. If it be objected that Mary's Borderland spouse was not an angel, but God himself, and therefore Borderland laws could be laid aside in His case, I reply that modern philosophy holds apparent miracles to be no violation of natural laws, but to have happened in accordance with some law as yet unknown to us; for God never breaks His laws, and if He became a Borderland spouse to Mary, it must have been in accordance with Borderland laws. And we, as made in His likeness, are bound by the same natural laws as God. Moreover, as Mary and me are sharers in a common humanity, she and me are bound alike, sharers in the glorious possibilities of Borderland...

[Missing portion of original manuscript].

...abraded survivals of an ancient religious teaching of marital purity and self-control of so lofty a type that it has been obscured by the fogs in the lowlands of modern sensuality.

Enlightened by my experiences as the wife of my unseen angel visitant, I wrote a defence (from a folklore standpoint) of the Danse du Ventre, which was published in the New York World.

This I afterwards added to, and issued in a typewritten essay for private circulation. As the essay showed that I wrote from experience, as I was still "Miss" Craddock, and as my social standing had hitherto been above suspicion, I deemed it only prudent to state to my readers that I had acquired my knowledge from a spirit husband. This I did on a little slip of paper pinned to the last page of the essay.

The persecutions which in consequence of this straightforward effort to tell the truth simply and clearly I suffered at the hands of those who deny the possibility of angelic communication, need not be dwelt on here. Suffice it to say that, while my non-occultist readers who did not know me personally pooh-poohed the idea of a spirit husband, declared that I must surely speak from an illicit experience, my non-occultist friends, who knew my habits of life from day to day, could find no explanation for the essay but that I must have gone crazy; and two physicians made efforts to have me incarcerated as insane.

One of the latter remarked: "Had that essay been written by a man, by a physician or by any other scientist (and the paragraph about spirit husband ommitted), it would have been alright; but coming from an unmarried woman, neither a physician nor a scientist, and with that claim of a spirit husband, there is no explanation possible but (1) illicit experience, which is denied by all who know her, or (2) insanity."

That is to say, because I had, by means of knowledge gained through channels of which he was ignorant, given utterance to what would have passed unquestioned if coming from a scientist, therefore, I must be insane! To put it more tersely a diamond of truth is to be considered genuine only when discovered by A or B; if the same diamond be discovered by X, Y, or Z, it is to be considered paste. My worst offence, however, in his eyes, seemed to be that, as a woman, I was out of my province in openly preaching marital reform, however high the ideals advocated; and, as my sense of duty did not conform with his conventional prejudices, he felt justified in seeking to incarcerate me until I should recant my heresy.

The factors in this case were:

1st. An unmarried woman of known reputation and integrity.

2nd. An essay written by that woman dealing with the marital relation along lines not known to one married couple in a thousand.

3rd. A claim by the essayist, that she wrote from an experience gained as the wedded partner of a ghost.

To ignore any one of these factors in arriving at a theory to explain the other two, is to invalidate that theory.

Now, there is one creed to which all genuine Freethinkers are faithful. It is to seek the truth, wherever it leads, and whatever the traditional belief upon the subject under investigation. This being so, I feel that I may confidently appeal to Freethinkers to consider carefully the evidence herewith submitted as to the world-wide extent of marital relations on the Borderland.

Last, but not least, I appeal to Spiritualists, Theosophists, and Occultists generally. Psychics and sex, Laurence Oliphant has shown, are so interwoven that you cannot take up one wholly separate from the other. Only an occultist—and somewhat experienced occultist, at that—knows anything of the perils which await the developing psychic on the Borderland. The Middle Ages are strewn with wrecked lives—mainly those of illiterate women who, beginning by dabbling with magic in an empirical fashion, ended by confessing themselves as witches, devil-haunted in body as well as in mind, and pledged to sins against nature.

Within the sheltered precincts of the most conservative of all Christian churches the Roman Catholic—really good and pious nuns have come under the sway of what the Church calls *"Congressus cum daemonis"*. And among the non-churchly practisers of modern occultism we too often find a tendency, on the one hand, not only to justifiable freedom, but also to unjustifiable looseness of life; or on the other hand, to a rigid asceticism and unnatural suppresion of the sex instinct as impure. All these things point to the necessity for some teaching as to the fundamental principles of sex morality on the Borderland—all the more, as spirit BRIDEGROOMS and spirit BRIDES are much more frequent than is generally supposed. Between the witch who held diabolic assignations as a devil's mistress, and the psychic who has been trained to self-controlled and reverent wedlock with an angel, it must surely be admitted, there is a wide stretch of road. Nevertheless, both are on the same road, and the downward grade is very slippery. In so far as I have been able to explore this road, therefore, I think it my duty to map out its perils and its safeguards, as to help my fellow occultists. For, no matter on what obscure by-path a psychic starts, he or she can never be sure of not coming upon this road unexpectedly, since it is, as I have said, one of the main thoroughfares of occultism.

To all three classes, then—to Occultists, Freethinkers, and Christians—I respectfully offer this treatise for consideration in the hope that each may find in it something of interest and, mayhap, of profit.

# HEAVENLY BRIDEGROOMS

THE celestial being who, whether as God or an angel, becomes the HEAVENLY BRIDEGROOM of an earthly woman, is better known to the literature of the Christian Churches than most people who are not theologians are aware. But he is not peculiar to Christianity. He has been known and recognized throughout the world in all ages. The woman to whom he comes is, as a rule, distinguished for her purity of life. Usually she is a virgin; but where already married and a mother, she must be recognized as chaste or, at least, there must be no stigma of impurity upon her reputation. I am not at the present writing aware of a single exception to this.

Let us, however, first consider the HEAVENLY BRIDEGROOMS of Christianity, from the popular orthodox standpoint.

There are two HEAVENLY BRIDEGROOMS — the Holy Spirit and Christ.

The first of these, the Holy Spirit, is, according to the New Testament, the Being through whose agency she whom the Catholic Church delights to honor as the Blessed Virgin became incarnate with Jesus. The second of these, Christ, is the Being honored alike by Catholics and by Protestants as the BRIDEGROOM of the Church; by Catholics also as the mystic Spouse of the ecstatic and purified nun, as in the case of Saint Teresa; and by

Protestants as the BRIDEGROOM of the Soul, in that popular hymn beginning:

> *"Jesus, Lover of my soul,*
> *Let me to Thy bosom fly!"*

I once attended a young women's revival meeting at Ocean Grove, held under the auspices of an evangelist who was noted for his success in converting young girls. When the enthusiasm flagged, and his hearers were slow in responding to his appeals to "come to Christ", he started the above hymn, and the ardor of his fair congregation was at once kindled, girl after girl rising to publicly give herself to Christ. That which earnest pleading for their soul's salvation had failed to accomplish, was brought about by this simple suggestion of the "Lover of the Soul". In thus stimulating the untrained emotions of a maiden to aspire to the Divine through symbolism of earthly affection, this revivalist not only showed keen insight into human nature, but was also instinctively true to the teachings of the innermost truth of all religions, as I hope to show further on.

In the Bible an entire book — the Song of Solomon — is given up to expressing the raptures of the HEAVENLY BRIDEGROOM and his BRIDE. At least, this is the interpretation which the Christian Church universally puts upon Canticles — the reciprocal joys of Christ, the

BRIDEGROOM, and His BRIDE, the Church.
Various phases of the sensuous relations of
husband and wife are there set forth in figurative but unmistakable terms of passion —
passion which the Christian world has, unfortunately, long since forgotten how to utilize as
the most important means of growth towards
the Divine.

But there are other HEAVENLY BRIDEGROOMS
besides Christ and the Holy Spirit referred to
in the Bible.

In the sixth chapter of Genesis may be
found a curious text, which reads:

> *"The sons of God saw the daughters of men, that*
> *they were fair; and they took them wives of all that*
> *they chose."*

The Septuagint originally rendered the
words 'Sons of God' by Αγγελοι Του Θεου,
angels of God, and this rendering is found in
Philo, de Gigantibus, Eusebius, Augustine
and Ambrose.

This view of Genesis VI 1-4 was held by
most of the early fathers.[*]

In fact, in the Book of Enoch, these sons of
God are spoken of all through as angels who
wedded earthly women; and it is further

---

[*] *See the Book of Enoch, translated from Professor*
*Dillman's Ethiopic Text by R.H. Charles, Oxford,*
*1893 e.v.*

stated that these angelic husbands broke the
law, living in depravity with their earthly
wives, and laying the foundation of evils
which required the Deluge to sweep away.
Critical scholarship usually holds these angels
to be fallen. But St. Augustine protests against
this view, saying: "I truly firmly believe that
God's angels could never fall so at that time."

Nevertheless, we find in the Book of
Enoch, XV 4:

> "Whilst you were still spiritual, holy, in the en-
> joyment of eternal life, you have defiled yourselves
> with women, have begotten (children) with the
> blood of flesh, and have lusted after the blood of
> men, and produced flesh and blood, as those
> produce who are mortal and short-lived."

Here we see that the angels, whatever their
after depravity, were "still holy" when they
united themselves as HEAVENLY BRIDEGROOMS
with earthly women.

However, from the above, and from other
texts in Enoch, it would appear that the angels
are blamed for having broken the laws of right
living so far as to turn the relations existing
between them and their earthly wives into the
grossest sensuality. They, rather than the
women, seem to be credited with the respon-
sibility for evil-doing. But it is noticeable that
Genesis is silent as to the character of these
angelic BRIDEGROOMS, while it lays stress on

the fact that the imaginations of men's hearts were evil continually, as though this last were the real cause of the wickedness which required the purification of the Deluge.

Now, let us remember that the Book of Enoch, although referred to in Jude, is not canonical. It belongs to the Hebrew Apocalyptic literature, and was for sometime lost, save for a few fragments preserved in references made by ecclesiastical writers. However valuable to scholars, it is uncanonical and thus cannot be accepted by Christians today as the Word of God. Genesis, on the contrary, is accepted by Christians today as the Word of God; and therefore, the total omission of this sacred book to bring any charge against these angelic "sons of God", while the depravity of man is dwelt upon at this period of the world's history, is not a matter to be passed over lightly by a Christian.

According to the Christian Scripture, then, it was not the wickedness of the angels who wedded earthly women, but the evil imaginations of the human heart that brought about the punishment of the Deluge. And in this, Genesis is in strict accord with modern Theosophy—the only philosophy, so far as I know, which professes to know the Alpha and Omega of occultism. Theosophy lays stress on the punishment which awaits the black sorcerer—the earthly being who uses real or pretended magical powers for evil purposes.

And not only the "black sorcerer" himself, but those who uphold him, share in the punishment dealt out by the Higher Powers—as the Theosophical Society has found, to its cost, when it attempted to shield both from public investigation and from Theosophic censure a member who was said to have fraudulently exploited a Mahatma to further his own interests.

But Theosophy is not alone in this teaching. All occultism, by whatever name it is called, however imperfect in deductions, learns at last to beware of the occultist who breaks the moral law, or who, whether wilfully or carelessly, through prejudice or through crafty desire to advance his own self-ish interests, closes his eyes to the truth. In other words, clear thinking and correct living are the only passport to trustworthiness in an occultist.

It is true that there are many psychical phenomena which at first sight do not seem to require any special exercise of morality on the part of the percipient. Such are the carefully attested phenomena of thought transference and wraith-seeing (especially of the astral form as "double" of people at the point of death or undergoing a sudden shock) which the Society for Psychical Research have collated from a multitude of sources—in the case of the "double" to the number of some three thousand. The percipients in these instances are probably average sort of folks, no better and no worse than the majority of their fellows. Yet they see or hear by means of senses which are still unrecognized by most people, and which are therefore termed "occult"; and what they perceived is afterwards proved to be an actual occurrence, often of something taking place miles away.

But it is to be observed that (1) the reliable cases collated by the S. P. R. are furnished by people who seem to be clear-headed enough, at least, to form definite mental conceptions; (2) that the majority of these cases are perceptions of occurrences in this earthly life. Where the thing claimed as seen or heard by the percipients no longer belongs to this world, but to the world beyond the grave, as in the case of visions or voices of those now deceased, the phenomena collated by the Society of Psychical Research seem not only to be accidental and capricious but they also seldom furnish a veridical (i.e., truth telling) communication.

In the case of Spiritualist mediums, professional or amateur, where the phenomena assume some show of regularity, and are claimed by the medium to come entirely from the world beyond the grave, one always has to be on one's guard against the subtle interpolation among otherwise truthful matter of fantastic or misleading statements made apparently by the communicating spirits themselves. Occultists in all ages have invariably assumed such statements to be the work of "lying spirits". But it is noticeable that a medium of correct life and clearness of intellectual conception is less troubled by such lying spirits than is the medium of halting intellect or morals. This of itself should indicate to the thoughtful student of occult phenomena that the medium, and not the spirits, may be to blame when lying communications are made. Just as in Astronomy it is now found that the apparent movements of the sun and fixed stars are due almost entirely to our own planet's motion through space, so, I think, when we explore the heavens of occultism we shall eventually realize that erratic psychical phenomena are due to our own shifting relation to the beings who produce phenomena. Not until people got rid of the Ptolemaic theory that the Earth was a permanent unmovable fixture in the heavens did they learn that the bewildering cycles and epicycles of the sun and fixed stars were caused by the movements of their own planet thorough space; and not until we get rid of what I may call the Ptolemaic theory of occultism, that the psychic is the one permanent, immovable factor in the apparently shifting phenomena about him, will we ever get at the true scientific laws of occultism that our own vibrations—or our own moral and intellectual ups and downs—are almost entirely responsible for the erraticness of Borderland communications. To blame Borderland intelligences for "lying" is as if in the proverbial London fog at noonday one should blame the sun for not shining. The sun is shining right along; but it is the smoke from one's neighbors which returns upon one to shield the sun from one's view.

It is generally assumed that the false or fantastic remarks so subtly interpolated into communications which are otherwise truthful and uplifting are due to the fact that evil spirits get temporary control of the medium. But this theory presupposes a state of society in the spirit-world far worse regulated than with us. It is often claimed, for instance, that crowds of spirits throng about a powerful medium as a crowd of people on earth sometimes flock about a telegraph operator in times of excitement, each man selfishly striving to get his message sent off first. But, even in our imperfect civic life, is such an occurrence usual? By no means. Is it likely that in a new life, with its added experience, such gross violations of law and order should be allowed to take place or to continue right along? By no means. Even if Heaven be not as Christian believe, the abode of God and the angels; even supposing that it is merely, as most Spiritualists claim, an improved edition of this world, it is but logical to infer that law and order will obtain there as here, and even more so, because the tendency of human society is always in the direction of systematizing its work for mutual convenience of its members. The idea that a good spirit may at any moment be temporarily displaced by an evil one, and that the laws of that clearer thought-world beyond the grave are powerless to cope with this annoyance is absurd, and contrary to common sense. The fault of imperfect communication is just as likely to be ours as theirs. Let us but see to it that the lines of psychical communication are laid (on our side of the abyss of death) in correctness of moral living, and clearness of intellectual conception before we rashly assume the fault to be theirs. If they are in a world where new laws of matter obtain, as they must be, if they live at all after the decay of the body, to communicate intelligently with us may not be as easy for them as we imagine. They may find themselves confronted at every turn by such difficulties as confront the traveler who seeks to explain to tribesmen the wonders of, say, the telephone or the phonograph. Between his mind and theirs, what a gap! And this gap cannot be bridged by the clearest of explanations of his part, unless the tribesmen in turn question and requestion on every point on which the least uncertainty remains. That is to say, the tribesmen must do their utmost to form clear intellectual conceptions of every idea set forth by their civilized visitor from afar, or he will leave their brains filled with the most ridiculous and distorted mind-pictures. Yet, the tribesmen and the civilized traveler are both dwellers on the same material plane, while the spirits who seek to tell us of the wonder of their life are evidently on a different plane of matter. How great the need, then, that we should take even more pains than must the tribesmen to form clear conceptions of every idea uttered by these visitors from an unknown land! One idea prejudged by us, and allowed to remain without due examination of the foundations on which it rests, will throw the remainder of our mental conceptions out of balance. One false theory, stubbornly held as gospel truth, places us mentally where all else is out of focus.

(Therein will be found also a statement requiring an occult principle which seems not only to forbid spirits from communicating accurately with an immoral medium, but which seems to positively enjoin upon them the utterance of all the foolish, depraved and even criminal ideas that the medium is willing to receive, and places us mentally at a standpoint where all else is out of focus. Thus, the slightest prejudices on any given subject under discussion between our celestial visitors and ourselves will render us liable to distorted conceptions of their ideas.) Such is the law of our own thought-world here on the earthly plane; and we must remember that they have left our plane and entered into a far wider thought-world than ours. Hence the need for rigidly clear thinking on the part of every would-be occultist. And, since, as has been well said, "All badness is madness", we must not forget to also reckon a well-ordered moral life as among the attributes of the really clear-headed man or woman. Thus, correct living and clear thinking go hand in hand as vouchers for accuracy of mediumship between this world and the world beyond the grave. The philosophy which deals with what is variously called the automatic faculty, the subjective consciousness, the subconsciousness or the sub-liminal ("Below the threshold") consciousness as an important factor in fantastic and misleading psychic phenomena from spirits will be found set forth at length in my little book on Hell's Happy Sunshine. Therein will be found a principle which seems not only to forbid spirits from communicating with an unworthy medium, but positively to enjoin upon them the utterance of all the foolish, depraved, and even criminal ideas that the medium is willing to receive. (Up to a certain point; beyond which the spiritual intelligences withdraw and the medium's own subconsciousness assumes control with the subterfuges and ingenious evasions peculiar to that faculty.) But when fantastic or misleading ideas emanate from spiritual intelligences and not from the medium's own

sub-consciousness, they are either as an ordeal for the training of the medium, or as a
wise and just punishment. To explain the application of this law in detail, however, would
extend the present treatise to an undue length.
Suffice to say here that in all such cases, however varied the manifestations, whether of a
super-normal sub-consciousness or of outside
intelligences, failure to think clearly, as to live
in accordance with the moral requirements of
self-control, duty, aspiration to the highest,
unselfishness and genuine purity, will be
found responsible for the disappointing psychic manifestations on the Borderland.

When, therefore, the Book of Enoch
blames the angelic sons of God, rather than
their earthly wives, for the depravity of relations said to exist between them as spirits and
mediums, we may well ask if this be not a matter on which the writer of the Book of Enoch
has carelessly accepted current legends. May
it not be that he, too, believed all depraved
psychical manifestations to be due to "evil
sprits", and that he was totally unaware of the
occult law which brings these things to pass
with a medium who, ignorantly but persistently, fails in clear thinking or correct loving?

Once more let us remember that the Book
of Genesis, which is canonical, lays stress on
the fact that at this epoch the imaginations of
men's hearts were evil continually.

Josephus refers to the subject as follows:

> *"For many angels of God accompanied with*
> *women, and begat some that proved unjust, and*
> *despisers of all that was good on account of the*
> *confidence they had in their own strength. For the*
> *tradition is that these men did what resembled the*
> *acts of those whom the Grecians call giants."*
>
> —Antiquities of the Jews I, iii.

Josephus it will be noticed, agrees with Genesis in laying no blame on either the angelic husbands or the earthly wives. Neither does he on their daughters. The sons, and only the sons, are denounced by Josephus as "despisers of all that was good", on account of the confidence they had in their own strength. His account, taken with that of Genesis, brings out a suggestive idea—that in the succeeding generations man was pre-eminently the sex which violated the laws of right living.

If this inference be warranted, the question arises: what were those laws of right living which the male sex violated to such an extent that a deluge was needed to purge the earth of their evil? The answer to this will be manifested further on.

When the Christian Church appeared on the stage of history, it found several varying traditions current about those sons of God who, so many centuries before, had taken unto themselves wives from among the daughters of men.

One after the other the early Church Fathers wrestled with these traditions, and strove to fit them into the Christian theological system. Beginning with Paul, we find that he asserts in the 11th Chapter of 1st Cor. that a woman ought to be veiled, as a token of her inferiority and dependence upon man, and he adds: "For this cause ought the woman to have a sign of authority on her head because of the angels." Irenaeus, in his work Against Heresies, quoting this text makes it read: "A woman ought to have a veil upon her head because of the angels." From Tertullian we learn what this "because of the angels" means. He says in his work Aganist Marcion (V. 18): "The apostle was quite aware that the spiritual wickedness (Ephesians, VI, 12.) had been at work in heavenly places when angels were entrapped into sin by the daughters of men."

In sundry places Tertullian waxes wroth over this supposed "entrapping" of angels by earthly women. In a treatise On the Veiling of Virgins—written as a rejoinder to those who claimed that women did not need to be veiled until they became wives, he speaks his mind thus:

> "So perilous a face, then, ought to be shaded, which has cast stumbling-stones even so far as heaven; that when standing in the presence of God, at whose bar it stands accused of the driving of the angels from their (native) confines, it may blush be-

*fore the other angels as well; and may repress that
former evil liberty of its head—a liberty now to be
exhibited not even before human eyes."*

                              —On Veiling of Virgins, VII.

The author of the Testaments of the
Twelve Patriarchs, is, if anything, more se-
vere. He remarks:

> *"Hurtful are women, my children; because,
> since they have no power or strength over the man,
> they act subtilly through outward guise how they
> may draw him to themselves; and whom they (do
> not) overcome by strength, him they overcome by
> craft. By means of their adornment, they deceive
> first their minds, and instil the poison by the glance
> of their eye, and then they take captive by their
> doings, for a woman cannot overcome a man by
> force. Therefore, my children, command your
> wives and your daughters that they adorn not their
> heads and their faces; because every woman who
> acteth deceitfully in these things hath been reserved
> to everlasting punishment. For thus they allured
> the Watchers before the flood."*

                              —Testament of Reuben, 5.

He adds that these angelic Watchers manifested as apparitions to the women at the
times of their union with their earthly husbands, "and the women, having in their minds
desire towards their apparitions, gave birth to
giants, for the Watchers appeared to them as
reaching even unto Heaven."

Here we see an attempt to account for the resulting progeny of "giants" spoken of in Genesis VI by such simple and natural means as Jacob made use of when he desired to produce "ring-straked, speckled and spotted" goats".\* No mention is made of marital relations being established directly between earthly women and angels. Elsewhere the same writer† speaks of these same Watchers as having "changed the order of their nature, whom also the Lord cursed at the flood, and for their sakes made desolate the earth."

This follows a reference to Sodom, the writer seeming to trace a similarity between the two causes of the two punishments. Justin Martyr, however, makes the offence of the sinning angels to consist rather in ambition for power over mankind. He says:

> "*God committed the care of men and of all things under heaven to angels whom He appointed over them. But the angels transgressed the appointment, and were captivated by love of women, and begat children who are those that are called demons; and besides, they afterwards subdued the human race to themselves, partly by magical writings, partly by fears and the punishments they occasioned, and partly by teaching them to offer sacrifices, and incense, and libations, of which*

---

\* *Genesis XXX*
† *See Testament of Naphthali, 3*

*things they stood in need after they were enslaved by their lustful passions; and among man they sowed murders, wars, adulteries, intemperate deeds, and all wickedness."*

These things, according to Justin, the poets (unaware that they were due to sinning angels) ignorantly ascribed to God (Jupiter) and to those who were called his brothers, Neptune and Pluto, and to the Olympian deities in general.

Lactantius lays the blame principally upon Satan. Speaking of the repeated efforts of the serpent ("who from his deeds received the name of devil, that is, accuser or informer") to corrupt mankind, he adds:

*"But when God saw this, He sent His angels to instruct the race of men, and to protect them from all evil. He gave these a command to abstain from earthly things, lest, being polluted by any taint, they should be deprived of the honor of angels. But that wily accuser, while they tarried among men, allured these also to pleasures, so that they might defile themselves with women. Then, being condemned by the sentence of God, and cast forth on account of their sins, they lost both the name and the substance of angels. Thus, having become ministers of the devil, that they might have a solace of their ruin they betook themselves to the ruining of men, for whose protecting they had come."*

—Lactantius: Epitome of the Divine Institutes

> *"Thus from angels the devil makes them to be-*
> *come his satellites and attendants. But they who*
> *were born from these, because they were neither*
> *angels nor men, but bearing a kind of mixed (mid-*
> *dle) nature, were not admitted into hell as their*
> *fathers were not into heaven. Thus there came to*
> *be two kinds of demnos, one of heaven, the other*
> *of the earth."*

—Ibid., II. 15.

In one place Justin Martyr speaks of "evil demons" who "in times of old, assuming various forms, went in unto the daughters of men." Elsewhere, he also speaks of these demons manifested as apparitions that misled boys as well as women.

He said that they "showed such fearful sights to men, that those who did not use their reason in judging of the actions done were struck with terror, and not knowing that these were demons, they called them gods." Justin evidently looks upon the angelic BRIDEGROOMS as demoniacal from the start. Clement of Alexandria says that the angels "renounced the beauty of God for a beauty which fades, and so fell from heaven to earth."

Athenagoras asserts that the angels "fell into impure love of virgins." And the author of the Clementine Recognitions says that they "fell into promiscuous and illicit connections." But Tertullian calls attention to the fact that sacred Scripture terms these angels husbands; and he argues at length very ably to show that we are bound to infer from Scripture that the earthly wives of these angelic husbands were virgins, pure and undefiled, at the time of their marriage. From which, I think, it is evident that these marriages were acceptable to virtuous women, and therefore, we may infer, not an infringement of the civil law of the time; or the sex which is proverbially conservative would never have contributed so largely to these unions from among its best members. Nor could they have been unions which transgressed the laws of nature, or the offspring which was said to have resulted would not have been so well developed physically (as giants) nor mentally (as "mighty men which were, of old, men of renown.")

Clement of Alexandria, in his Miscellanies (*Stromata*), appears to blame the sinning angels in addition because they "told to the women the secrets which had come to their knowledge; while the rest of the angels concealed them, or, rather, kept them against the coming of the Lord." These "secrets", we learn from several of the Christian Fathers, were the arts of metallurgy, dyeing, the properties of herbs, astronomy and astrology, etc. Reasoning from this assumption—that certain sciences and industrial arts were imparted to mankind from sinful angels, we need not wonder that Tertullian pertinently asks:

*"But, if the self-same angels who disclosed both
the material substances of this kind and their
charms—of gold, I mean, and lustrous stones—and
taught men how to work them, and by and by in-
structed them, among their other instructions, in the
virtue of eye-lid powder and the dyeing of fleeces,
have been condemned by God, as Enoch tells us,
how shall we please God while we joy in the things
of those angels who, on these accounts, have pro-
voked the anger and vengeance of God?"*

— Tertullian on Female Dress, II. 10.

This thought seems to have been to him a
matter of serious moment, for he enlarges
upon it as follows when speaking of the dress
and ornamentation of women:

*"For they, withal, who instituted them are as-
signed, under condemnation, to the penalty of
death—those angels to wit, who rushed from heaven
on the daughters of men; so that this ignominy also
attached to women. For when to an age much more
ignorant (than ours) they had disclosed certain well-
concealed material substances, and several not well-
revealed scientific arts—if it is true that they had laid
bare the operations of metallurgy, and had divulged
the natural properties of herbs, and had promulgated
the powers of enchantment, and had traced out every
curious art, even to the interpretation of the stars—
they conferred properly and as it were peculiarly
upon women that instrumental means of womanly
ostentation, the radiance of jewels wherewith necklaces are variegated, and the circlets of gold*

*wherewith the arms are compressed, and the medicaments of archil with which wools are colored, and that black powder itself wherewith the eyelids and eyelashes are made prominent. What is the quality of these things may be declared meantime, even at this point, from the quality and condition of their teachers; in that sinners could never have either shown or supplied anything conducive to integrity, unlawful lovers anything conducive to chastity, renegade spirits anything to the fear of God. If these things are to be called teachings, ill masters must of necessity have taught ill; if wages of lust, there is nothing base of which the wages are honorable. But why was it of so much importance to show these things as well as to confer them? Was it that women without material causes of splendor, and without ingenious contrivances of grace, could not please men, who, while unadorned and uncouth, and—so to say—crude and rude, had moved the minds of angels? Or was it that the angelic lovers would appear sordid and—through gratuitous use—contumelious, if they had conferred no compensating gift on the women who had been enticed into connubial connection with them? But these questions admit of no calculation. Women who possessed angels as husbands could desire nothing more; they had, forsooth, made a grand match. Assuredly they who of course did sometimes think whence they had fallen and, after the heated impulses of their lusts, looked up towards heaven, thus requited that very excellence of women, natural beauty, as having proved a cause of evil, in order that their good fortune might profit them nothing but that, being turned from simplicity and sincerity they, together with the angels them-*

*selves, might become offensive to God. Sure they were all that ostentation and ambition, and love of pleasing by carnal means, was displeasing to God."*
            —Tertullian on Female Dress, Ch. II.

Cyprian, when blaming virgins for wearing jewels, necklaces and wool stuffs colored with costly dyes, likewise remarks:

*"...All which things sinning and apostate angels put forth by their arts, when, lowered to the contagions of earth, they forsook their heavenly vigor."*
            — On the Dress of Virgins, 14

When we remember that early Christianity set its face like a flint against all delights of the senses, and that this extreme reaction of the spiritual against the sensuous has largely shaped our social customs of today, we begin to see how important and far-reaching were these opinions of the early Church Fathers that feminine adornment had been taught by angels who had sinned in wedding earthly women, and that it was therefore a sinful thing in that it had emanated from a depraved source. Some of the theories built upon this assumption are quite curious. Here are a few:

*"That which He Himself has not produced is not pleasing to God, unless He was unable to order sheep to be born with purple and sky-blue fleeces: if He was able, then plainly he was unwilling; what*

*God willed not, of course, ought not to be fash-
ioned."*

— Tertullian on Female Dress, I. 8.

*"For it was God, no doubt, who showed the way
to dye wools with the juices of herbs and the humors
of conchs; it had escaped Him, when He was bidding the Universe come into being, to issue a
command for the production of purple and scarlet
sheep."*

— Ib., II. 10.

*"Why should she walk out adorned? Why with
dressed hair, as if she either had or sought for a husband? Rather let her dread to please if she is a virgin.
It is not right that a virgin should have her hair
braided for the appearance of her beauty."*

— Cyprian on the Dress of Virgins, 5.

*"You are bound to please your husbands only.
But you will please them in proportion as you take
no care to please others. Be ye without carefulness,
blessed sisters; no wife is ugly to her own husband.
She pleased him enough when she was selected by
him as his wife; whether commended by form or by
character. Let none of you think that if she abstain
form the care of her person (compositione sui) she
will incur the hatred and aversion of husbands.
Every husband is the exactor of chastity; but beauty
a believing husband does not require, because we are
not captivated by the same graces which the Gentiles
think to be graces."*

— Tertullian on Female Dress, II. 4.

*"O good matrons, flee from the adornment of vanity!*
*Such attire if fitting for women who haunt the brothels.*
*To a wife approved of her husband, let it suffice that*
*she is so not by her dress, but by her good disposition."*

— The Instructions of Commodianus in favor of
    Discipline against the Gods of the Heathens.

Let us remember that these and similar
teachings by the early Christian Fathers have
laid the foundation of our present marriage
customs. The theory that a woman sins in
adorning herself to please a husband (whether
present or prospective) is still indescribably
popular among devout Christians.

Commodianus ascribes the teaching of
"arts, and the dyeing of wool, and everything
which is done", not to the angels but to the
giant progeny. And he adds:

*"To them, when they died, man erected images.*
*But the Almighty, because they were of an evil*
*seed, did not approve that, when dead, they should*
*be brought back from death. Whence wandering*
*they now subvert many bodies, and it is such as*
*these especially that ye this day worship and pray*
*to as gods."*

— Ibid

The author of the Clementine Homilies
records a tradition concerning these gigantic
"wanderers" on the borders of Ghostland
which seems to be that they were not unable

to beget children. After speaking of the
Deluge, he says:

> "Since, therefore, the souls of the deceased gi-
> ants were greater than human souls, inasmuch as
> they also excelled their bodies, they, as being a new
> race, were called also by a new name. And to those
> who survived in the world a law was prescribed by
> God through an angel, how they should live. For
> being bastards in race, of the fire of angels and the
> blood of woman, and therefore liable to desire a
> certain race of their own, they were anticipated by
> a certain righteous law."
>
> — Clementine, Homilies, VIII, 18.

Inasmuch as the Deluge had already destroyed every one on the earth except Noah
and his family, we see that the author cannot
mean by those who survived in the world any
giants still in the flesh. Moreover, the decree
which follows and which prescribes that they
were to have power over only those human
beings who broke the moral law and practiced
magic would indicate these "giants" had then
entered upon what Theosophists would call
the astral; and from the paragraph quoted
above, it is evidently taken for granted that
these astral giants would propagate their kind.
This is an important point—the testimony of
a Christian Father of a tradition that human
beings (not created angels) who had once in-
habited bodies, could beget children on the
plane of the astral unless prevented by the di-

rect prohibition of Heaven. If it be objected
that the author refers to giants still in earthly
form when he speaks of "those who survived
in the world", I am sure that the statement follows a remark about the Deluge and that in
that case the surviving giants must have been
Noah and his family. This view, however, is
absurd, when we consider that the decree forbade the giants to assume power over any but
the human race. If Noah and his family were
the surviving giants, where would be the
sense in promulgating such a decree to them?
This same author gives an account of the doings of the angelic fathers of these giants
which reminds one of the spirit seances of the
late Rev. Stainton Moses, when under conditions which precluded all fraud or illusion tiny
pearls and other precious stones suddenly materialized before the sitters.

Here is the tradition recorded by the
Christian Fathers:

>    "For of the spirits who inhabit the heaven, the
> angels who dwell in the lowest region, being grieved
> at the ingratitude of man to God, asked that they
> might come into the life of man, that, really becom-
> ing man, by more intercourse they might convict
> those who had acted ungratefully towards Him,
> and might subject every one to adequate punish-
> ment. Then, therefore, their petition was granted;
> they metamorphosed themselves into every nature;
> for, being of a more god-like substance, they were

*able easily to assume any form. So they became*
*precious stones, and goodly pearl, and the most*
*beauteous purple, and choice gold, and all matter*
*that is held in most esteem. And they fell into the*
*hands of some, and into the bosoms of others, and*
*suffered themselves to be stolen by them. They also*
*changed themselves into beasts and reptiles and*
*fishes and bird, and into whatsoever they pleased.*
*These things, also, the poets among yourselves by*
*reason of fearlessness sing, as they befall, attrib-*
*uting to one the many and diverse doings of all."*

— Clementine, Homilies, VIII, 12.

Then, "having assumed these forms, they
convicted as covetous those who stole them,
and changed themselves into the nature of
man, in order that, living holily, and showing
the possibility of so living, they might subject
the ungrateful to punishment."

However, "having become in all respects
men, they also became subject to masculine
infirmities, and fell."

Does it not seem as though we had here a
survival of Animism—a state of mind frequent
among tribesmen, children and animals, in
which an inanimate object which moves without visible cause or manifests in any peculiar
way is thought to be alive? A horse is often
terrified by a piece of paper blown in front of
him; evidently he takes it for a live creature.
Tribesmen speak of the sun and moon as living individuals because of their apparently
voluntary journeys through the sky; among

the Kukis of Southern Asia, if a man was killed by a fall from a tree, his relatives would take their revenge by cutting the tree down, scattering it in chips. A modern King of Cochin, China, when one of his ships sailed badly, used to put it in the pillory, as he would any other criminal. °In classical times, the stories of Xerxes flogging the Hellespont and Cyrus draining the Gyndes occur as cases in point, but one of the regular Athenian legal proceedings is yet a more striking relic. A court of justice was held at the Prytaneum, to try any inanimate object, such as an axle, a piece of wood or stone, which had caused the death of anyone without proved human agency; and this wood or stone, if condemned, was with solemn form cast beyond the border. The spirit of this remarkable procedure reappears in the old English law (repealed in the present reign) whereby not only a beast that kills a man, but a cart-wheel that runs over him, was forfeited and sold for the poor. The pathetic custom of "telling the bees" when the master or mistress of a house dies, is not unknown in our own country. In Berlin, Germany, the idea is more fully worked out; and not only is the sad message given to every beehive in the garden, and every beast in the stall, but every sack of corn must be touched and everything in the house shaken, that they

---

* *Bastian, Oestl., Asein, Vol 1, p. 51.*

may know the master is gone.* And we all know that even an intelligent nineteenth century man is not above administering an angry kick to a chair against which he has bruised himself.

Now, the author of the Clementine Homilies seems to have similarly lighted on an instance of Animism in connection with gold, pearls, precious stones, etc. In prehistoric times this tradition, rational and intelligible, may suppose that these precious articles had moved or otherwise behaved as though endowed with life in the ancient times to which the tradition relates. Could it be that they suddenly appeared to those prehistoric gazers, coming from no one knew where, and moved about by unseen hands? As tables are lifted, bells rung, banjos played or flowers materialized at a modern Spiritist seance? As they were reputed to have come by occult means, supposed to be heavenly. The people who witnessed the phenomena were probably not accustomed to clear-headed and intelligent investigation of such phenomena. One sees at once it was an Animistic explanation such as is given in the Clementine Homilies. As to the frightened horse, and to the tribesmen, inanimate things seem to be alive, so may the precious objects which materialized at those

---

* Tylor, Primitive Culture, I 286-7.

prehistoric seances have seemed to the amazed beholders to be living creatures, inasmuch as they sped through the air without visible support. If alive, they surely (so would argue the witnesses) must be angelic beings, since they were said to come from heaven; and the attendant phenomena of the seance no doubt would increase the awe with which these "angels" were received and treasured. An "angel" is simply a vehicle for a message, in the original signification. Let us glance in passing at the accounts of materializing through the psychic power. In this sense, a pearl materialized through the psychic power of so reliable a modern medium as the Rev. Stainton Moses, plainly by occult means, might be called an "angel"—i.e., the means by which the message from the unseen reached the sitters. In after times, when the word angel had come to be specialized as a personal envoy from Heaven, the old tradition about the pearls and precious stones which had evidently come as "angels" (vehicles for a heaven-sent message), whenever told, would probably be adopted to the specialized meaning and it would be said, as above, that personal beings transformed into those inanimate things. First, as to the manifestations through the Rev. Stainton Moses lately declared in his journal, occurs the following entry:

*Tuesday, September 9th, 1873*

"*Same conditions. Plentiful scent as before. Sixteen little pearls were put on the table, six having been previously given during the day. Mrs. Speer and I were writing at the same table, and a pearl was put on my letter as I was writing. After that I saw a spirit standing by Mrs. Speer, and was told that it was Mentor, who had put a pearl on Mrs. Speer's desk. After that four others came. They seemed to drop on the table, just as I have seen them with Mrs. A—h. We have in all twenty-two now. They are small seed pearls, each perforated.*"

A week later, there is this entry:

"*When we broke up we found a little heap of pearls was put before each. One hundred and thirty-nine little pearls have been brought to us, one hundred and ten in the last two days.*"

(This, it appears from another witness, occurred in daylight.)

Dr. Speer (referred to by Miss X. in Borderland as "a highly intelligent and by no means credulous witness") gives a striking instance of the materialization of a precious object:

*December 31st, 1872*

*"A very successful seance. A blue enamel cross was brought, no one knew whence, placed before my wife, who was told to wear it."*

Mrs. Speer testifies as follows:

*Ventnor, November 29, 1893*

*"I wish to state that the most convincing evidences of spirit-power always took place when hands were held.*

*"Other manifestations occurred, often in light, such as raps, raising of table, scent, musical sounds, and showers of pearls. Two cameos were carved in light while we were dining."*

Before leaving this part of the subject, it may be well to quote the following by Miss X. in Borderland. (Miss X., I would add, is by no means a spiritualist, but is distinctly opposed to the Spiritistic hypothesis):

*"Mr. Stainton Moses has for many years been one of the most important witnesses for Spiritualism. The fact that, like Professor Crookes and Alfred Russell Wallace, he was a gentleman, a scholar, and a man of recognized position and character, was, to say the least, a good letter of introduction. It may be said, once for all, that it is unnecessary to insist on the absolute sincerity of Mr. Stainton Moses. It is a point which has never been so much as raised. His life has been of a kind not to be called in question—obscure without*

*mystery, dignified without pedantry, lived in the sight of just that class of the public which demands the strictest respectability of conduct, the most un-equivocal correspondence between life and profession. As a clergyman, he was beloved by his parishioners, as a schoolmaster he was respected by his boys, and as a personal friend he com-manded the confidence and esteem of all his intimates."*

May it not be that the phenomena rec-orded by the author of the Clementine Homilies are essentially the same in kind as those referred to above in the case of the Rev. Stainton Moses?

St. Augustine, considering the possibility of occult sex relations between earthly women and beings from the unseen world, remarks:

*"The Scriptures plainly aver that the angels have appeared both in visible and palpable figures. And seeing it is so general a report, and so many aver it either from their own experience or from others, that are of indubitable honesty and credit, that the sylvans and fauns, commonly called incubi, have often injured women, and that certain devils from the Gauls called "Duses" do continu-ally practice this, and tempt others to it, which is affirmed by such persons, and with such confidence that it were impudence to deny it.*

*"I dare not venture to determine anything here; whether the devils being embodied in air (for the air being violently moved is to be felt) can suffer this lust, or move it so as the women with whom*

*they commix may feel it; yet do I firmly believe that*
*God's angels could never fall so at that time."*
— St. Augustine's City of God, XV, 23.

Notice the perplexity of St. Augustine as a logician. He cannot deny that occult sex relations exist on the Borderland, the testimony to this is too widespread and of too reliable a character. But (we can imagine him saying), how to reconcile these phenomena with the popular belief that the inhabitants of the world beyond the grave are immaterial, vapory, mist-like beings?

How can such a hazy, ethereal creature as a ghost produce objective sensations of touch upon an earthly being? And if possible—as he ingeniously supposes, by such means as air becomes perceptible to us when violently put in motion—how reconcile such phenomena with the belief that sex is impure, and that it does not exist in the world beyond the grave? How could God's angels ever fall so? It were impossible!

But St. Augustine evidently starts from two hypotheses—the insubstantiality of ghosts and the impurity (footnote, as will be seen by a perusal of the quotation in full), and, therefore, non-existence of sex, neither of which two hypotheses has ever been definitely proven. As a logician, therefore, he is at fault, and I have already shown the danger of starting from mistaken premises when dealing with occult phenomena. The two hypotheses, however, were not peculiar to St. Augustine. They were, and are, the common property of the majority of mankind. But it does not follow that they are correct: and the psychic who rashly assumes their truth to start with (through prejudice or because other people think so) may expect to be deluded, and to come upon all sorts of fantastic, and possibly diabolical, manifestations. Such is the occult law. Start with a false premise or with a premise which you have not investigated with scrupulous care, and you are certain to get phenomena of either a misleading or a depraved character.

But all the Christian Fathers did not accept the possibility of BRIDEGROOMS from the unseen world. There were then, as now, materialist minds which disbelieved in ghosts. Alexander, Bishop of Lycopolis, endeavored to explain away angelic BRIDEGROOMS as myths, thus:

> "When the Jewish history relates that angels came down to hold intercourse with the daughters of men, this saying signifies that the nutritive powers of the soul descended from heaven to earth."
> — On the Tenants of the Manicheans

Hence the "injuring" of women by incubi—to which St. Augustine refers, an injuring either wholly subjective and illusory, or, if objectively real, was brought about in part by the woman's ignorance of the occult requirements of correct living and clear-headedness on the Borderland, in part by her failure to thus live and think on the earthly plane.

It would be interesting to know his authority for this. Rationalistic theories cannot rest, as do folklore traditions, upon a mere say-so; they must be supported either by testimony or by argument. Otherwise, we are obliged to dismiss them as the whimsical fancies of a solitary individual.

Origen says he will "persuade those who were capable of understanding the meaning of the prophet, that even before us there was one who referred this narrative to the doctrine regarding souls, which became possessed with a desire for the corporeal life of men" and thus in metaphorical language he said were termed "daughters of men". But Origen does not give his authority, nor advances any argument in support of this explanation.

Julius Africanus suggests another Rationalistic explanation, but is candid enough to give it as his own notion. He says:

> "When men multiplied on the earth, the angels of heaven came together with the daughters of men. In some copies I find 'the sons of God'. What is meant by the Spirit, in my opinion is that the descendants of Seth are called the sons of God on

*account of the righteous men and patriarchs who have sprung from him even down to the Saviour Himself; but that the descendants of Cain are named the seed of men, as having nothing divine in them, on account of the wickedness of their race and the inequality of their nature, being a mixed people, and having stirred the indignation of God."*

This ingenious theory has been eagerly grasped at by succeeding Christian writers who disbelieve in the substantiality of ghosts. So able a commentator in modern times, however, as Delitzsch (*On Genesis*) decides against this view, and quotes various authorities which I give elsewhere. He also quotes Keil as demonstrating that two of the Hebrew words in the text in Genesis show that "the contraction of actual and lasting marriages" is meant.

Julius Africanus, indeed, seems to have had doubts as to whether the current tradition about angelic BRIDEGROOMS might not be true after all, for he adds directly upon the heels of the above theory:

*"But if it is thought that these refer to angels, we must take them to be those who deal with magic and jugglery, who taught the women the motions of the stars and the knowledge of things celestial, by whose power they conceived the giants as their children, by whom wickedness came to its heights on the earth, until God decreed that the whole race*

*of the living should perish in their impiety by the
Deluge."*
— Extant Fragments of the Five Books of
   the "Chronography of Julius Africanus"

Nevertheless, Rationalists and Materialists
are in the minority among the Fathers of the
"Church" as regards this subject. The majority accepted the accounts in Genesis and
Enoch at their face value.

To briefly sum up the majority's views of
early Christianity on this matter:

1. Angels of a superior order did come into
the earthly life—whether (a) because God
sent them, or (b) because they were moved
with indignation at the ingratitude of men toward God and came voluntarily in order to
reconcile God and man, or (c) because they
were enticed by women on the earth, the traditions do not agree.

2. Having come into this earthly life, they
became either the lovers or the husbands of
women, whether beguiled thereto in part by
the Devil, or wholly by the women or, partially or wholly by their own desires, the
traditions do not agree. One tradition, as we
have seen, hints at the sin of Sodom; and an
interference on the astral plane with the rights
of earthly husbands; others hint at illicit
amours; but Tertullian demonstrates unan-
swerably from sacred Scripture that the
angels were the wedded husbands of the

daughters of men, and that these daughters were virginal at the time of wedding their angelic lovers.

This was not, however, all their sin. One tradition, as we have seen, makes a vague allusion to the sin of Sodom in connection with the intercourse of angels with women.

3. That an angel should seek a woman in honorable marriage, specially an earthly woman, it would appear, was reckoned a sin. When asked why, we find that the "Church" Fathers, one and all, treated marriage as a mere expedient. Tertullian said that the reason why 'marrying' is good is that 'burning' is worse. Minneius Felix (Octavius XXXI) remarks that "with some, even the modest intercourse of the sexes causes a blush."

Methodius has an entire book devoted to an argument offered by ten virgins against wedlock and in behalf of perpetual virginity. Origen says: "God has allowed us to marry, because all are not fit for the higher, that is, the perfectly pure life." Cyprian says that "Chastity maintains the first rank in virgins, the second in those who are continent, the third in the case of wedlock". He also says:

> "What else is virginity than the glorious preparation for the future life? Virginity is of neither sex. Virginity is the continuance of infancy. Virginity is the triumph over pleasures. Virginity has not children; but what is more, it has contempt for off-

*spring; it has not fruitfulness, but neither has it bereavement; blessed that it is free from the pain of bringing forth, more blessed still that it is free from the calamity of the death of children. What else is virginity than the freedom of liberty? It has no husband or master. Virginity is freed from all affections; it has not given up to marriage, nor to the world, nor to children."*

— Cyprian, Of the Discipline of Chastity

Justin Martyr exults that "many, both men and women of the age of sixty and seventy years, who have been disciples of Christ from their youth, continue in immaculate virginity."

In a spurious fragment credited to "Hippolytus, the Syrian Expositor of the Targum", the writer refers to an ancient Hebrew MS., which tells of Noah being commanded by God to stake off each male animal in the ark "for the sake of decency and purity"! The Church Fathers generally held that the one object of the marriage institution is to bear children. The other principal object of marriage, which runs through all nature from protoplasmic cells up to man — of mutual exchange of strength and mutual happiness — seems to have been totally ignored by the early Christian Fathers. Lactantius held that it is impossible the two sexes could have been constructed except for the sake of generation. Justin Martyr says frankly:

*"Neither marry at first, for no other object than to rear children, or else abstaining from marriage continue to live in a state of continence."*

— Apology I, 37

He notes with approval a Christian youth who begged Felix, the governor of Alexandria, for permission to be made a eunuch by a physician, in order to attest his continence to the world. (Felix, however, had the good sense to refuse.) To such an extent was this unnatural loathing for wedlock carried, that Constantine found it judicious to remove the old-time penalties against celibacy, because of the many Christians who continued celibates from motives of religion.

Since marriage on natural grounds was thus deprecated by the early Christian Church as impure when occurring between earthly men and women, we need not wonder that she viewed with horror the very thought of wedlock with an angel, inasmuch as angels were supposed to be above earthly weaknesses. Having thus started from a false premise, i.e., that marital passion cannot be pure in God's sight, there was no other deduction to be made regarding these love-matches between angels and women but that they were sinful.

4. But, according to the Christian Fathers, the angels committed other sins, in addition to seeking a woman in honorable marriage. They

actually endeavored to beautify the world into which they had come, and to make men wiser and happier by teaching them various arts and sciences!

One might have thought this a cause for gratitude; but the Church Fathers, having started from a false premise, were logically bound to deduce the theory which Tertullian did—that as these spirit husbands were fallen angels, what they taught could not possibly be conducive either to integrity, chastity, or the fear of God. Therefore, dress and adornment and the industrial arts of dyeing and metallurgy were sinful, and consequently, displeasing to the Almighty. Very different is the view taken by a more modern writer, Sir Thomas Browne, the author of the Religio Medici, who, advocating the doctrine of this celestial guardianship over marriage on earth, observes:

> *"I do think that many mysteries ascribed to our own inventions have been the courteous revelation of spirits; for these noble essences in heaven bear a friendly regard unto their fellow natures on earth."*
> —Apparitions, pp. 3-4.

5. Ambition plays a prominent part in the traditions, it will be noticed. It is said that these angels were ambitious for earthly power and exacted libations and sacrifices; and also

that they were the beings whom the heathen ignorantly supposed to be gods.

But if the reader will recall what I have said about the misleadings in spirit manifestations when the psychic starts from a false premise, he will understand how possible it is that we have to deal here with subjective illusions, and not objective realities; and that the lower estimate in which these angelic visitors came to be held was due entirely to the failure of earthly psychics to keep the laws of correct moral living or common sense; then, weaknesses and vanities and superstitions will be played upon ad libitum. As for the giant offspring said to have resulted from these unions—offspring which in the male line became evil-doers, and finally demons on the astral plane—if the reader will consider that necessity to which I have referred for correct living and clear thinking on both sides of the abyss of death, if the bridge of communication is to hold, he will see that if these "giants" continued to influence the world from the astral plane they could not be evil demons, but must be beneficient helpers of mankind. But there is, I think, grave doubt as to whether such offspring ever resulted from these unions between angels and earthly women, as the reader will see when I come to speak of the occult laws governing such unions. Nevertheless, there is something to be said on both sides, and we should do well to reserve our judgment until all the evidence is before us.

We have seen that Commodianus says that these giants are the gods to whom the heathen ignorantly prayed.

Justin Martyr, mindful of certain similarities between the stories told of those same heathen gods and the scriptural account of Jesus, advances the theory that the demons had some imperfect perception of the coming Messiah, gleaned from the Old Testament prophecies, and that they tried to forestall Christianity by ascribing Christ's possible attributes in advance to the gods. Justin says:

> *"The demons, then, hearing these prophetic words (Genesis 49: 10, 11), asserted that Bacchus was born the son of Jupiter; they ascribed to him also the invention of the vine, and in the celebration of his mysteries led an ass in procession, and taught that Bacchus was torn in pieces and taken up into heaven."*
>
> — Justin Martyr's Apology, I. 71

Justin also draws a comparison between some of these gods and Christ, to show that Christianity claims no more for its god than did the heathen for those whom they called "Sons of Jove". He says:

> *"When we affirm that the Word, which is the first-begotten of God, was born without carnal*

knowledge, even Jesus Christ our Master, and that he was crucified, and rose again and ascended into heaven, we advance no new thing different from what is maintained respecting those whom ye call sons of Jupiter. For ye well know how many sons your approved writers attribute to Jupiter: Mercury, the word of interpretation and teacher of all men; Esculapius, who was a physician, and yet was struck with lightning and taken up into heaven; Bacchus, who was torn in pieces; Hercules, who burned himself upon the pyre to escape his torments; Castor and Pollux, the sons of Leda; Perseus the son of Danae; and Bellerophon, born of human race, and carried away upon the horse Pegasus. Neither is it necessary that I should relate to you, who already know well, of what kind were the actions of each of those who were called the sons of Jupiter; I need only say, that the writings in which they are recorded tend only to corrupt and pervert the minds of those who learn them; for all take a pride in being the imitators of the gods. But if we say that he (Jesus) was begotten of God, in a manner far different from ordinary generation, being the Word of God, as we have before said, let this be considered a correspondence with your own tenets, when ye call Mercury the word who bears messages from God. And if any one objects to us that He was crucified, this too is a point of correspondence with those whom ye call the sons of Jupiter, and yet allow to have suffered. Again, if we affirm that he was born of a virgin, let this be considered a point in which he agrees with what you (fabulously) ascribe to Perseus. And whereas we say that he made those whole, who were lame, {480} palsied and blind from their birth, and raised the *dead; in this too we ascribe to him actions similar to those which are said to have been performed by Esculapius.*

— Justin Martyr's Apology I, 28, 29, 30

We thus see that the heathen gods and heroes whose father was Jupiter, the Christian Messiah whose father was the holy spirit and the traditional "giants" whose fathers were angels were, in the eyes of at least one Church Father, but different aspects of the same underlying principle: the possibility of marital union between dwellers in the unseen world and dwellers upon the earth, for the purpose of begetting children.

Today, however, we look upon the story of the virgin-born Perseus as fabulous. But the ancient heathen opponents of Justin seem to have accorded as scant respect to the story of the virgin-born Jesus as we do to the story of virgin-born Perseus. Now, to laugh to scorn the birth of Perseus from the occult union of God with one virgin, and then to accept without question the birth of Jesus from the occult union of God with another virgin, is somewhat inconsistent.

On strictly logical grounds, if one story be false, so may the other be false; if one be true, so may the other be true. But Perseus is only one of many virgin-born heroes or gods. We find these children of a visible earthly mother and an invisible, celestial mysterious father the world over, in all ages.

There was Buddha, the child of Maya and a celestial god being who, in the form of a white elephant, entered her side; or, according to De Gingnes*his mother conceived by a ray of light, and without defilement.

The Hindu Chrishna was born of a chaste matron who, though a wife and a mother, is always spoken of as the Virgin Devaki. Chrishna, by the way, has many attributes in common with Kama, the East Indian god of love, corresponding to the Latin Cupid. He is represented as black—a symbolism to which I will return later on.

The Egyptian God Ra was born from the side of his mother, "but was not engendered".

The Mayas of Yucatan had a virgin-born god, named Zama.

Among the Algonquin Indians we find the tradition of a great teacher, by name Michabou, who was born of a celestial Manitou and an earthly mother.

"Upon the altars of the Chinese temples were placed behind a screen images of Shin-Moo, or the 'Holy Mother', sitting with a child in her arms, in an alcove, with rays of glory around her head, and tapers constantly burning before her." (Rev. Joseph B. Gross, Heathen Religion, 60, quoted in Bible Myths,

---

* See Higgins, Anacalypsis I, 157.

p. 327.) Shin-Moo is called the "Mother Goddess", and the "Virgin".

In ancient Mexico, "the virgin Chimalman,
also called Solchiquetzal or Suchiquecal, was
the mother of Quecalcoatle (evidently the
same as Quetalcoatl, who was crucified as a
Saviour for the Mexicans, as Jesus was for
the Christian world.)

In one representation he is shown hanging
by the neck holding a cross in his hands. His
complexion is quite black.

Sochiquetzal means the lifting up of Roses.
(This is really our Sukey, and the Greek
$\Psi\theta\chi\eta$], Psyche, which means the soul, and
which was appropriately applied to the BRIDE
of the spirit-lover, Cupid.) Eve is called
Ysnextli, and it is said she sinned by plucking
roses. But in another place, these roses are
called Fruta del Arbor (arbol?).

"The Mexican Eve is called Suchiquecal. A
messenger from heaven announced to her that
she should bear a son, who should bruise the
serpent's head. He presents her with a rose.
This was the commencement of and Age,
which was called the Age of Roses."

(Is this the age when angels became the
husbands of pure-minded women—an age
fitly symboled by the rose, the flower of perfect love? Note, also, the resemblance
between this tradition and the Christian tradition, concerning the angel's offering Mary a
lily-branch at the Annunciation. Evidently,

these are two different aspects of the same symbolism.)

Higgins, continuing, says: "All this history, the monkish writer is perfectly certain is the invention of the Devil" and Justin Martyr strove to account for the analogy between the story of Christ and the story of Bacchus by supposing that demons had imitated the Christian Scriptures in advance, so totally unaware was he that both stories had the same esoteric meaning to the initiate. Torquemada's Indian history was mutilated in Madrid before it was published.

Suchiquecal is called the Queen of Heaven. She conceived a son, without connection with a man, who is the God of Air.

*"The Mohammedans have a tradition that Christ was conceived by the smelling of a rose."*
                        — Anacalypsis II, 32, 33.

In the Finnish epic of the Kalevala there is a heroine by the name of Mariatta (from Marja, "berry") who becomes pregnant through unwittingly eating a berry—the berry here played a similar part to the rose referred to above in the Mohammedan tradition. She goes from one to another person, vainly seeking a place in which to bring forth her child. At last she is referred by one household to the stable of "the flaming horse of

Hisi", and she then appeals to the horse of
Hisi in the following words:

> "Breathe, O sympathizing fire-horse,
> Breathe on me, the virgin-mother!
> Let thy heated breath give moisture,
> Let thy pleasant warmth surround me,
> Like the vapor of the morning:
> Let this pure and helpless maiden
> Find a refuge in thy manger!"

Observe that, although the mother of an
illegitimate child she, like all the mothers of
such children when their father is divine or
mysterious, is "pure", the "virgin-mother",
etc.

These virgin-mothers are not copies of the
Christian Mary. Most, if not all of them, were
known long before the days of Christianity.

The mother of the Siamese Somona
Cadom was impregnated by sunbeams,
another form of Danae's golden shower. She
was called Maha Maria or Maya Maria, i.e.,
"the Great Mary". And this brings out some
curious coincidences in name among virgin-
mothers. Thus:

Marietta of the Kalavala has already been
referred to above.

The mother or Hermes or Mercury was
Myrrha or Maia.

Maya, the mother of Buddha, is identical
in name with the Hindu goddess Maya, who

is represented as walking upon waters, with her peplum teeming with animals, to show her fecundity. Maya is also a well-known Hindu term for "illusion".

The month of May (so nearly like the name of Maia) was sacred to some of the virgin-goddesses of ancient times, as it is now to Mary, the Mother of Jesus. The Christian Virgin Mary was also called Myrrha and she is still called Santa Maria in Southern Europe and in Mexico. The title bestowed on her of "Star of the Sea"—a title given to the Egyptian Virgin-Mother, Isis, perhaps two thousand years earlier—shows how close a resemblance tradition and folklore have traced between both of these virgin-mothers and the ancient genitrix of the waters. Also, the Latin "mare" and the French "mer" for "the sea" and the French "mere" for "mother" bear a striking resemblance to the name Mary in sound. And Venus, the presiding divinity of love between the sexes, was born from the foam of the sea. She is credited with having been "indulgent Venus" to a mortal man, Anchises, to whom she bore the hero of Virgil's Aeneid; a Borderland espousal, this, though here it is the wife and not the husband who comes from the invisible world.

The Apocryphal Gospels speak of the Virgin Mary's being brought up as an orphan, in the temple, and they refer to her as an obe-dient and pure-minded maiden, accustomed to holding daily converse with angels. That she should have been called by the same root-name as these ancient virgin-mothers is, therefore, the less remarkable, if we consider the possibility of her having been trained in the temple by the priests as an initiate in the sacred mysteries, and of her having passed the various ordeals so successfully as to entitle her to be called by the name sacred to the type of womanhood worthy to sustain marital relations on the Borderland.

In some cases it would appear that ambitious princes or other designing politicians of ancient days did not scruple to avail themselves of the current belief in the possibility of divine paternity, when it would serve their purpose. It was an open secret among the Greeks that Alexander the Great had not hesitated to do this, on the occasion of his march into Egypt and Syria, when the oracle at the temple of Jupiter Ammon (doubtless for a bribe) declared Alexander to be the son of Jupiter, saying that this god, in the form of a serpent, had manifested to Alexander's mother.

The serpent is, in ancient sex worship, a well-known symbol of the phallus, and therefore of the creative fatherhood. It appears in several stories of divinely begotten children.

Scipio Africanus was another politician who availed himself of the popular belief in these matters, it would seem. "There is no doubt," remarks Higgins in his Anacalypsis, I, 212,-213, "that he aimed at the sovereignty of Rome, but the people were too sharp-sighted for him." A. Gellius says, "The wife of Publius Scipio was barren for so many years as to create a despair of issue, until one night, when her husband was absent, she discovered a large serpent in his place and was informed by soothsayers that she would bear a child. In a few days she perceived signs of conception, and after ten months gave birth to the conqueror of Carthage."

The Emperor Augustus was said to have been the result of a mysterious connection of his mother with a serpent in the temple of Apollo.

Ovid in his Fasti records a story that Servius Tullius was son of a mysterious shape, claiming to be a vulcan, which appeared to the mother, Ocrisia, among the ashes of the altar, when she was assisting her mistress (Ocrisia was a captive) in the sacred rite of pouring a libation of wine upon the altar.

Pythagoras, who lived more than five hundred years before Christ, was said to be the offspring of Apollo. He was born on a journey, his father (or rather, his mother's earthly husband) having traveled up to Sidon on business. Pythais, the mother, had been beloved by a ghostly personage who claimed to be the god Apollo. Afterwards this same apparition showed itself to the husband, informing him of the parentage of the coming child, and bidding him to have no connection with his wife until after its birth.

A similar event is said to have transpired in the case of Plato, Apollo his father also. His mother was Perictione, a virgin, who was betrothed to one Ariston at the time. In this case also Apollo appeared to inform the earthly lover of the child's paternity. Higgins, relating this tradition, adds:

> "On this ground, the really very learned Origen defends the immaculate conception (Higgins evidently refers not to the Roman Catholic doctrine of Mary's stainlessness signified by that term, but to the conception of Jesus) assigning, also, in confirmation of the fact, the example of Vultures (Vautours) who propagate without the male."

The Vulture was an accompaniment of Hathor, the Egyptian Venus; and it would therefore seem as though Origen had unwittingly stumbled on a bit of folklore. Graves, in his Sixteen Crucified Saviors, remarks (I know not on what authority, but give his remark rather for its suggestiveness than as a vouched-for historical fact):

> "Many are the cases noted in history of young maidens claiming a paternity for their male offspring by a God. In Greece it became so common that the reigning King issued an edict, decreeing

*the death of all young virgins who should offer such an insult to deity as to lay to him the charge of begetting their children."*

*"The tradition of the Vestal Virgin Rhea Sylvia, who bore Romulus and Remus to the god Mars, is well known. It is a curious coincidence that the name Rhea, which was one of the names of the Mother of all the gods, is applied by one writer to the Virgin Mary, who likewise became the `Mother of God'".*

The Mongolian conqueror, Genghis Khan, and his two twin brothers were said to be the result of an occult union of the earthly mother with a mysterious intelligence.

*"His mother having been left a widow, lived a retired life, but some time after the death of her husband she was suspected to be pregnant. The deceased husband's relations forced her to appear before the chief judge of the tribe for this crime. She boldly defended herself, by declaring that no man had known her; but that one day, lying negligently on her bed, a light appeared in her room, the brightness of which blinded her, and that it penetrated three times into her body, and that if she brought not three sons into the world she would submit to the most cruel torments. The three sons were born, and the princess was esteemed a saint. The Mongols believed Genghis Khan to be the product of this miracle, that God might punish mankind for the injustices it had committed."*

—Anacalypsis II, 353

Of the conqueror Tamerlane, who claimed direct descent from Genghis Khan on the mother side, it is related that he was the result of a connection of his mother with the God of the day.

Dean Milman says, in his History of Christianity (Bible Myths, p. 119):

> *"Fo-hi of China—according to tradition—was born of a virgin, and the first Jesuit missionaries who went to China were appalled at finding, in the mythology of that country, a counterpart of the story of the Virgin of Judaea."*

But, had those same Jesuit missionaries apprehended the idea which lies back of both stories—the substantiality of the unseen world beyond the grave and the possibility of marital relations on the borderland of that world and this, they would not have been thus "appalled". The mother of Confucius, says one tradition, while walking in a solitary place, was impregnated by the vivifying influence of the heavens.

The Chinese philosopher, Lao-Tse, born 604 B.C., the founder of the Religion of the Supreme Reason, was said to have been born of a virgin of black complexion—a forerunner this, by hundreds of years, of the Black Madonnas in the Italian Churches.

Do those black madonnas typify, mystically, the darkness of the unknown world beyond the grave whence the Heavenly Spouse emerges?

The Earls of Cleave were said to descend from a union between the heiress of Cleave and a being from the upper air, "who came to Cleave in a miraculous ship, drawn by a swan, and after begetting divers children `went away at Noon-day, in the sight of a World of People, in his Airy Ship.'"

The famous Robert le Diable, according to one tradition, was the child of an incubus.

The enchanter Merlin, "son of an incubus and of a holy woman, became the center and the master of all nature", says Peyrat. The Magic of the Middle Ages, Rydberg, speaks of a number of adventurers during the Middle Ages who asserted themselves or others to be the bastards of devils and human beings. If they led a blameless life, evincing a firm belief in the dogmas of the Church, the danger of such a pedigree was not greater than its honor. The son of a fallen angel did not need to bend his head before a man of noble birth.

"But," it will be objected, "these stories are myths of ancient, or at least, mediaeval, times. You don't find virgin-born children nowadays."

Stay!

In the establishment of Schweinfurt, that individual in Rockford, Illinois, who today claims to be the Christ, a woman a few years since bore a child, and steadfastly declared her belief that it was immaculately conceived. Trial, it is said, before a jury of the women of Schweinfurt's establishment, did not succeed in shaking the faith of these women in the possibility of such a thing.

In the Truthseeker of New York occurs this paragraph:

> *"Mrs. Helen Fields, of Wichita, Kansas, has given birth to a child whose father she avers is the Holy Ghost."*

Moncure D. Conway, in his Demonology and Devil-Lore, II. 231, says:

> *"When in Chicago in 1875 I read in one of the morning papers a very particular account of how a white dove flew into the chamber window of a young unmarried woman in a neighboring village, she having brought forth a child, and solemnly declaring that she had never lost her virginity."*

It is, of course, easy to dismiss all these stories, ancient, mediaeval and modern, with contempt, as so many falsehoods or, at best, self-delusions. I have already said that, despite the immense number of traditions and miraculous births, I doubt if such ever occur upon the borderland of the two worlds, owing to certain occult principles to which I shall briefly refer further on. Nevertheless, this mass of folklore belief is too overwhelming in quantity and too widely diffused to be dismissed lightly. Back of it all there must be some objective realities and some fire for all this smoke. And we must not forget that there is one miraculous birth which is accepted throughout Christendom—the birth of Jesus from a Divine Father and an earthly Virgin Mother. Nevertheless, by the cultured heathen opponents of Justin the story of the divine paternity of Jesus seems to have been regarded with a scorn similar to what with which we regard the above tales today; and that Church Father showed his wisdom when he placed heathen and Christian stories upon the same logical basis.

Am I not right in saying that to impugn the possibility of marital relations between earthly women and HEAVENLY BRIDEGROOMS is to strike at the very foundations of Christianity?

In folklore customs and fairy tales, fantastic though these may be, we find numerous indications of the world-wide belief in BRIDEGROOMS and BRIDES from the unseen world of spiritual beings; or, as they were termed in the middle ages, incubi and succubae. (Latin, *incubo,* "to lie upon"; *succubo,* "to lie under".)

We may set out with that description among the islanders of the Antilles, where they are the ghosts of the dead, vanishing when clutched; in New Zealand, where ancestral deities 'form attachments with females, and pay them repeated visits'; while in the Samoan Islands such intercourse of mischievous inferior gods caused 'many supernatural conceptions'; and in Lapland, where details of this last extreme class have also been placed on record. From these lower grades of culture the idea may be followed onward. Formal rites are specified in the Hindu Tantra which enable a man to obtain a companion—nymph—by worshipping her and repeating her name by night in a cemetery.

Congress with ghostly beings is mentioned in the bull of Pope Innocent VIII in 1484, as an accepted accusation against "Many persons of both sexes, forgetful of their salvation, and falling away from the Catholic faith". [*]

Among the Metamba negroes, a woman is bound hand and foot by the priest, who flings her into the water several times over with the intention of drowning her husband, a ghost, who may be supposed to be clinging to his unfeeling spouse.[†]

In China, it is not considered respectable for widows to re-marry, for the express reason that their husbands are expected to return to them from the world beyond the grave and

---

[*] Taylor, ibid.
[†] T. F. Thiselton Dyers, The Ghost World, p. 182.

resume marital relations with them upon the Borderland.

In the case of widows it would appear to be but a resumption of a relation previously established between the two upon earth. And there are indications that the same stress is not laid upon passing preliminary ordeals as in the case with the virgin, who "has never known man". May it not be because of the virgin's greater ignorance, physiologically speaking, so that she has to enter upon a more extended course of training than does the widow, who already has experience?

The myths and fairy tales which speak of maidens with mysterious lovers from the realm of the unseen are certain to contain, so far as I have observed, reference to some rule or pledge which the woman must strictly observe. If she fails to do this, her lover vanishes, and she can find him again only after passing long and toilsome ordeals. Such was the case with Psyche, who broke the command of her heavenly lover, Cupid, not to look upon him while he slept. He had come to her night after night in the darkness, unseen, as is the wont with so many of these HEAVENLY BRIDEGROOMS; and she naturally desired to see his face. But, in her eagerness to know him more intimately, she let fall a drop of hot oil from the lamp upon him, which awoke him, and he vanished. This myth is an evident euphemism for a broken law of marital self-control. In other words, she wanted to enter upon the second step in the occult training which she was receiving from her husband, before she had fully mastered the first step. What those steps were—first, second and third—(for there is a third) through which the earthly wife of a HEAVENLY BRIDEGROOM must will appear further on in this book.

In one of the oldest of the Vedas—those books which contain the legends of the Aryans before they split up into fragmentary races—we find a similar story about Urvasi and Pururavas.

These two stories are usually explained as myths which show how the dawn vanishes as soon as it looks upon the sun. In solar myths, the dawn is often typified as a maiden, the sun-god being her lover who pursues her vanishing form through the heavens—an idea picturesquely brought out in the myth of Cinderella. If these two stories really are a bit of sun and dawn folklore, then Urvasi and Psyche must each be the dawn-maiden, and Pururavas and Cupid must be the sun-god on whose glorious form, unveiled by any clouds, the dawn-maiden dare not look, for, as she looks, the two lovers become separated—i.e., the dawn vanishes before the rising sun. But it is a little curious that in one story the maiden disappears, while in the other it is the lover himself who flees. Obviously there is some other myth than a purely solar one involved in these two stories — stories so strikingly similar and yet so strikingly at variance in the one feature in which they should agree, if true sun and dawn myths.

May not their likeness be due to their being memorials of the belief in Borderland marriages and in the self-control which is obligatory upon the earthly partner in such marriages? May not their unlikeness as to the sex of the partner who disappears when that self-control is violated be due to there being heavenly BRIDES, as well as HEAVENLY BRIDEGROOMS?

To these same myths, I take it, belong all those fairy stories of which Beauty and the Beast is the type. Here, a maiden noted as a rule for her amiability and gentleness is served each day by invisible hands, and at night receives her lover, in the form of a handsome prince. By the ordinary light of day, he is a monster, appalling to behold, or, in some of the stories, he is invisible; but night and the marriage couch cause him to materialize in his true shape. Finally, her family and friends — themselves quite outsiders as to these experiences — work upon her feelings and make her believe that this union is evil (in occult parlance, it would be termed diabolical) and she breaks off her connection with him. In the end, true love triumphs, and the lovers are reunited under happier auspices — that is, in the fairy story; in actual life, it too often happens that Beauty and the Beast are permanently separated by meddling outsiders who ignorantly assume that everything which they cannot understand comes from the Devil. The poor earthly psychic has so constantly dinned into her ears the fact that her mediumship has revealed glimpses of monstrosities and deceptions that she comes at last to fear lest her invisible visitor be in truth the evil demon which at times, by the sober light of day, he seems to be. All unaware of the law by which her own failures and peccadilloes bring about subjective hallucinations which mislead, she ascribes to her angelic BRIDEGROOM a tendency to evil which he does not possess, and finally comes to shrink from him as demoniacal. And the laws of Borderland forbid his undeceiving her so long as she holds to her prejudice as if it were gospel truth. Thus Beauty too often turns away from her princely lover forever, so far as this earth-life is concerned, as Beauty in the fairy story did from the husband whom ignorant outsiders had led her to look upon as Beast.

Pyramus and Thisbe, the lovers who, separated by a huge wall, were fain to satisfy themselves with kisses exchanged through a hole therein, are a euphemistic expression for those marital unions one of the parties to which is invisible to his earthly love, impalpable to the physical senses. In this story a bloodthirsty lion puts an end to the love-making. This is probably the solar lion, the meaning being that the ancient faith is superseded by the later and (in some respects) purer Sun Worship which seems to have been a reform movement of the science and materialism of the time against the Borderland sensuality which obtained in the declining age of Sex Worship.

Isis and Osiris are also types of the husband and wife who united upon the Borderland. Egyptian sacred traditions were wont to relate that Osiris was killed by the evil Typhon, who then cut up his victim's body into fourteen pieces, enclosed it in an ark, and set it adrift upon the River Nile. Isis, the Virgin-Mother, sought far and wide for these remnants of her husband's body. One legend states that she found all, except the phallus; another, that she found nothing except the phallus, and from that solitary fragment she reconstructed her husband, entire. Here we evidently have two sides of the same esoteric idea—that the loss of sex power constitutes the true death of the soul (not, of course, the spirit) and that in the finding of one's marital partner on the Borderland the ghost may be gradually materialized into substantiality by beginning at the same starting-point as did Isis.

HEAVENLY BRIDEGROOMS, it will be noticed, predominate over heavenly BRIDES in Borderland traditions. The reason, I take it, is

that women, because of their social environment, usually lead a more self-controlled and
temperate life than men do, and thus are in
most (though not all) respects more worthy of
marital union with an angel. Custom allows
men more freedom—a privilege which the
masculine sex is not slow to avail itself of,
especially in the direction of wine, women and
tobacco. These three dissipations not only ex-
haust the nerve force of men, but blunt both
their physical and their moral sensibilities so
that the man for whom, in all possibility, his
angel mate may be waiting upon the
Borderland may find himself handicapped at
the outset, should he ever essay an adventure
into Borderland romance while still on the
earth. In this connection, we may remark that
in India, where the attempt to obtain a spirit
wife is said to be of common occurrence (and,
it would appear, often rewarded with success)
we find a nation singularly gentle and peace-
able in disposition, unaccustomed to
drunkenness until taught it by outside peoples
(there is a proverbial saying among the
Hindus, "as drunk as a Christian") and endowed by nature with a tendency to aspire to
union with God. Last, but not least, it is a
nation whose religions, for the most part,
recognize the truth that sex is holy; and in this
it is in strong contrast with our Western
"civilization" where the most sacred function
of humanity is looked upon as vile. We

occidentals have a whole life's teaching to unlearn, before we can approach the subject of marital relations on the Borderland from a natural and pure-minded standpoint.

The chief tradition regarding spirit BRIDES relates to Lilith or Lilis or Lilot, and is mostly Rabbinical. As in the case of the angelic BRIDEGROOMS, she is supposed to be demoniacal. Lilith is said to have been Adam's first wife; one tradition says that by her he begat only demons, another says that she rebelled when Adam assumed authority over her and fled from him to the evil angel Samael, to whom she bore a demon progeny. Another legend has it that being jealous of Eve she slipped back into Eden behind the particeps criminis in the temptation.

Another says that Adam kept himself apart from Eve for a hundred and thirty years in order not to fill hell with their offspring; but that in a weak moment a female devil, called Lilith, seduced him and became his wife, and from their union arose devils, ghosts and evil night dreams; and Eve in like manner became the wife of a demon. (The Serpent in Paradise, London.) Of a similar tenor is the tradition about the Zoroastrian Yeina, who fell from a state of innocence by means of a great serpent, the Azis-Dahaka.

For a long period Yena and his subjects were in the power of this evil serpent, Azis-Dahaka. Yena himself, in order to oblige this master, had to abandon his own wife, who was also his sister, and to take a female devil for his wife, and consent to the union of his former wife with a demon. From these unions were produced apes, bears, and black men."

During this evil period women much preferred young devils to young men for husbands, and men married young seductive "Paris", or female devils.

The psychic who can sustain marital relations on the Borderland must above all be sensitive at the extremities of the nerves of touch. Neither blind people nor deaf people are hindered by their respective infirmities from marrying in this earth-life; and on the Borderland a psychic may be clairvoyant and clairaudient to only a limited extent, and yet be a partaker in connubial joys. For the Borderland husband must materialize more or less fully to enable her to understand the relation clearly upon the physical side. Whereas for most men this is unnecessary, and the spirit BRIDE may remain in all save a few essentials invisible, inaudible, intangible—a veritable "woman of air". Hence her ghostliness and her philological connection with the idea of pale blue or pale purple—the color of air and the mist.

Lilith is said to come to young men's bedsides at night to seduce them, under the aspect of a beautiful and finely dressed woman with golden hair. And, afterwards, she strangles them, and they are known to be Lilith's victims because one of her golden hairs is found tightly wound around the victim's heart. In the Zoroastrian legends, she is much connected with night and night dreams; and men are cautioned not to sleep alone for fear of the evils of Lilith.

She also lies in wait for children to kill them if they are not protected by "Amulets".

*"Herodotus says that the Arabians called the moon Alilat. The Assyrian word for night is Lilat, and Talbot supposes that the Arabians really called the moon 'Sarrat ha Lilat', the queen of the night.*

*"Mr. Talbot also says 'Alilat' may also mean the star Venus.*

*"The Greeks considered Lilith evidently to be the moon, as with them she is Ilithyia, the sister of Apollo, one of the birth goddesses. Night in Hebrew is layelah.*

*"That the moon should be selected to represent the feminine principle is readily accounted for by her waxing and waning propensities, to say nothing of her controlling or coinciding with the feminine periods."*

— The Serpent in Paradise, etc.

Summing up these varying traditions we find the following incidents prominent:

1. A woman who is not of the earth but evidently from an unknown world enters upon relations with Adam or with the men of later generations.

2. The relation is in most cases that of husband and wife and not a mere liason.

3. In those cases where the relation is illicit, the earthly partner comes to an unfortunate end.

4. This woman from the unseen world is credited with being a seducer and a devil.

5. She bears no children, save demons, and is reputed to destroy children.

6. She causes men to dream evil dreams at night.

Lilith is evidently the complement of the tradition about angelic BRIDEGROOMS. That the typical spirit BRIDE should have so much more unsavory a reputation than has the typical spirit BRIDEGROOM is also typical of nowaday. The masculine nature is proverbial for its lack of self-control where women are concerned; and in this it has usually contrasted unfavorably with the self-control of women in similar cases. On the other hand, the men of our Western civilization are mostly superior to our women (of the virtuous classes) in the ardent, dramatic and artistic expression of love for the opposite sex—a desirable qualification in the romance and uncertainties and trying ordeal of Borderland wedlock.

If, therefore, the propositions which I have laid down as to the necessity for self-control in occult investigations be correct, we need not be surprised that the spirit BRIDE is ere long denounced as demoniacal and seducing.

But it is the ignorance or the wilful wrong-doing of her earthly lover that is to blame, and not the spirit-BRIDE—unless in some rare instance, where the celestial visitor is exceptionally careless. In that case, her superiors in the invisible world interfere and remove her. The connection with her earthly partner is snapped, never to be resumed until he passes over to her world at death. But such failures on the part of the heavenly visitor are rare; and if the resulting phenomena are diabolical, it is the earthly medium's own fault.

That she should bear no children except demons points to the proposition which I have already advanced, that children cannot be begotten from Borderland marriage unions. If the earthly husband still insists on doing all he can to beget such children he breaks the law of Borderland, and will be led deeper and deeper into the mire of sensuality, and at last, perhaps, be deceived by a subjective hallucination of devils whom he will be told are his children. If he presses for information, he will probably receive a more explicit truthful statement, i.e., that his spirit BRIDE is unable to bear children on the Borderland of two worlds. But should he fail about this time in some detail of moral duty, or clear-headedness, and especially should he persist in sowing seed where no harvest can be reaped, he will most certainly be misled by all sorts of fantastic excuses. For such is the occult law. The psychic who, whether ignorantly or wilfully, is unworthy, loses his grip on the lines of communication, and his own ill-regulated subliminal consciousness then steps in with its ingenious excuses — such as, perhaps, that his celestial partner is abnormally constituted as a woman, or that she kills her children as fast as they are begotten, etc. etc. And thus, through the failure of the earthly husband to observe the laws of marital self-control on the Borderland, one more tradition is launched upon the world about the devil-BRIDE who seduces men and begets demons and kills children.

That she should be credited with being the author of "evil night-dreams" shows how prone the partners of spirit BRIDES have been to subjective hallucinations. We do not find any such wholesale charge brought against spirit husbands of producing evil dreams, as is brought against Lilith. The imaginations of men's hearts must indeed have been evil in those days, and their brains beclouded, or the difference between a materialized spirit BRIDE and the subjective phantasm of an amorous dream would have been more sharply defined. The psychic who conforms two separate planes of existence has forsaken the path of self-control and clear-headedness, and has entered upon the path whose end is insane delusion.

In the supplement of Littre's Dictionary (French), 1877, occurs a suggestive etymology of the lilac (or as it is in French, *lilas*). The writer connects the root of this word with the Persian *nil*, indigo, and calls attention to the various Persian words *nilah, niladj, liladj, lilandj, lilang,* all relating to indigo. He connects the word *lilas* (French for lilac) with these words and also the diminutive lilak (bluish, as fingers blued by the cold) — a tint which perfectly characterizes the flowers of the lilac of Persia which are of a plae purple. May there be some philosophical connection between this palely purple flower *"lilas"* and the ghostly *"Lilis"* or *"Lilat"* or "Lilith"?

Lilith figures in a text of Isaiah, but we have to go both to Mohammedan and to Ancient Greek folklore to find the connecting link between this text and the Lilith of Rabbinical traditions. The text refers to the destruction which the Lord threatens will befall Eden, and reads:

*"And thorns shall come up in her palaces,
nettles and thistles in the fortresses thereof; and it
shall be an habitation of jackals, a court for
ostriches and the wild beasts of the desert shall
meet with the wolves (or howling creatures); and
the satyr (or he-goat) shall cry to his fellow: yea,
the night monster shall settle there, and shall find
her a place of rest".*

— Isaiah XXXIV 13-14

The word "night-monster" is in Hebrew
"Lilith". The King James version translates
this word "screech-owl"; the Vulgate,
"Lamia"; in Luther's Bible, "Kobold". Lamia
or Lamya is found in the Great Bible, and in
Coverdale's, Matthew's, Beck's and Bishop's
bible.

Now a lamia is a mythical serpent-woman
of a demoniacal character. Philostratus, in his
Life of Apollonius of Tyana, gives a memora-
ble instance. A young man on the road near
Corinth met a charming woman who invited
him to her house in the suburbs of the city,
and said that if he would remain with her, "he
should hear her sing and play, and drink such
wine as never any drank, and no man should
molest him and she being fair and lovely
would live and die with him." The young man
was, as Burton in his Anatomy of Melancholy
puts it in giving the account, "a philosopher,
otherwise staid and discreet, able to moderate
his passions, though not this of love" and he
"tarried with her awhile to his great content."

At last he married her. To the wedding came
Apollonius, and he at once recognized her as
a lamia, and declared that all her furniture
was but illusion. She wept and begged
Apollonius to be silent, but he persisted in exposing her, whereupon she, her house, and its
content, vanished.

This is probably a Beauty and the Beast
myth on the masculine side, Apollonius play-
ing the part of the outsider who separates the
lovers by harping on the things which are
illusory and monstrous in the young man's
psychic manifestations. It is worth noticing, in
this connection, that the young man had been
living a temperate and self-controlled life
when he was first approached by this Lamia
or Lilith, so that he was evidently found
worthy to taste the joys of affectionate connubial intercourse with his mysterious BRIDE.
Here, evidently, the young man is not strong
enough to endure the training required to
consummate Borderland wedlock. He also,
evidently, does not have his sub-consciousness well under control, but allows it to run
away with him. Mastery of self in every possible    aspect,    physically,    intellectually,
morally,    affectionately,    is    one    of    two
requisites for sustained marital relations on
the Borderland; the other requisite being
steadfast aspiration to personal communion
with the Divine.

The ancient Churchyard of Truagh, county Monaghan, in Ireland, is said to be haunted by an evil spirit, whose appearance generally forebodes death. The legend runs, writes Lady Wilde:

> "—That at funerals the spirit watches for the person who remains last in the graveyard. If it be a young man who is there alone, the spirit takes the form of a beautiful young girl, inspires him with ardent passion, and exacts from him a promise that he will meet her that day month in the churchyard. The promise is then sealed by a kiss, which sends a fatal fire through his veins, so that he is unable to resist her caresses, and makes the promise required. Then she disappears and the young man proceeds homewards; but no sooner has he passed the boundary wall of the churchyard than the whole story of the evil rushes on his mind, and he knows that he has sold himself, soul and body, for a demon's kiss. Then terror and dismay take hold of him, till despair becomes insanity, and on the very day month fixed for the meeting with the demon BRIDE the victim dies the death of a raving lunatic, and is laid in the fatal graveyard of Truagh."

—T.F. Thiselton Dyer's "The Ghost World"

In Capt. Richard F. Burton's translation of the Arabian Nights occurs a story of a female desert-monster, who devours human flesh. Captain Burton, in a footnote, remarks:

*"The Ghulah (fem. of Ghul) is the Hebrew Lilith or Lilis; the classical Lamia; the Hindu Yogini and Dakini; the Chaldean Utug and Gigim (desert-demons) as opposed to the Mas (hill-demon) and Telal (who steal into towns); the Ogress of our tales and the Baba-yaga (Granny-witch) of Russian folklore. Etymologically 'Ghul' is a calamity, a panic fear; and the monster is evidently the embodied horror of the grave and the graveyard."*

In its more usual spelling of "Ghoul", this graveyard monster will probably be familiar to most readers.

*"The female Ghul appears to men in the deserts, in various forms, converses with them, and sometimes prostitutes herself to them."*

Here we see (1) the spirit BRIDE, degraded to the level of harlot, (2) vague and unreasoning terror, (3) loathing and horror of the spirits of the deceased, all meeting under one name. So far has Lilith, the Borderland BRIDE, fallen from her rightful estate by reason of the befogged imaginations of mankind.

*"The Shiqq is another demoniacal creature, having the form of a half human being (like a man divided longitudinally) and it is believed that the Nasnas is the offspring of the Shiqq and a human being. The Nasnas is described as having half a*

*head, half a body, one arm, and one leg, with
which it hops with much agility."*
— A Dictionary of Islam, *Genii*

This is another form of the giant progeny
of Borderland unions, a form so fantastic as to
show that its origin is a subjective hallucination, and not an objective reality. In other
words, the Mohammedan Shiqq and Nasnas
are both of them probably the subliminal invention of some imperfect earthly psychic in
the centuries agone, who broke the
Borderland law in his or her relations with a
spirit BRIDE, or a spirit husband, and who was
grossly midled, in consequence, by his or her
own subliminal self. That others since then
claim from time to time to see these fantastic
creatures does not prove that they exist. In
psychical matters nothing is more common
than for people to see ghosts at a given time
and place when their imaginations have been
worked up to the expectation of seeing one
then and there, of a certain predetermined
type.

The Mohammedan Paradise as well as its
Borderland recognizes love between the
sexes. And in this it differs from the Christian
paradise as popularly conceived — although,
as I have elsewhere shown, the statement by
Jesus that we shall be after death, as regards
marrying, "like the angels in heaven", when
taken in connexion with the text in Genesis

about the sons of God who wedded earthly women, shows pretty conclusively that the Christian Scriptures admit the existence of sex and marriage in the world beyond the grave. Nevertheless, the Romish Church has chosen to flatly contradict the teaching of both the Old and the New Testament in this, with the result of blinding Christians utterly to these potent Scriptural truths. Mohammed, on the other hand, was sufficient of a seer to venture on restoring the ancient doctrine.

Heaven, as is well known, abounds in love-making, beautiful women called Houris attending upon the risen soul of the male Mohammedan as he reclines at feast. It is true that apologists have suggested a figurative sense in which the accounts of Mohammed's Paradise are to be taken.

On the contrary, it is not at all remarkable. It was precisely because Mohammed was at that time living a fairly well-ordered and self-controlled life that he was enabled to learn sufficiently of the world beyond the grave to assert that love between the sexes survives death and is one of the potent factors in social life there, as here. It is true that, being an Oriental, his "revelations" would inevitably conform to his cast of mind, so that the glitter and luxurious abandon of a feast presided over by Houris might seem to him the acme of ideal bliss. But beneath and permeating all this voluptuous imagining breathes the mighty truth of sex-love in Paradise.

That love which mutually strengthens and mutually uplifts as no other love in all the world can strengthen and uplift. I take it is the chief reason for its existence—the propagation of the species being of necessity incidental, therefore, secondary.

But there is also a third reason which, unfortunately, is known to but few. Nor is it likely to be understood as it should be until modern civilization ceases to brand the sacred details of the marriage union with the stigma of impurity. The third reason for the marital union is that for those who are worthy, it is, whether on the Borderland or the earthly plane, the surest and safest method of seeking union with the Divine Heart of the Universe and becoming one with all God's world. Only in giving joyful thanks to God, indeed, should that relation ever be entered upon, whether on the Borderland or on the earthly plane. This, not only because it is fitting to give thanks to God for every good thing, but because it is beautiful at that time and because only those who have experienced the bliss of taking God into the marital partnership in its most intimate relation can be said either to be truly wedded or to truly realize what it is to love God and be in return beloved by Him. This applies in earthly as well as Borderland wedlock.

Trite and commonplace as may seem this suggestion, to give thanks to God in this relation and share one's joy with Him, it nevertheless appears to be the inner, sacred truth of all religions on their esoteric side, and of all mysticisms and forms of occult teaching, the world over—a truth which has been jealously hidden away from the masses. It has been concealed for several reasons, probably.

First, it is not a matter to be attained at once, but requires systematic and careful training in self-control. And some degree of intellectual and spiritual insight is necessary to rate this training at its just value, as well as to respect the sacredness of the idea which underlies it. There are three degrees to be passed in this training, of which I will speak later on.

Second, inasmuch as it enhances, instead of extinguishing, connubial pleasure, while at the same time it puts the begetting of children absolutely under the control of parents, and this without violation of either civil or natural laws, its initiates evidently feared lest it be turned to base uses by the unscrupulous and licentious. A needless fear, this, however; as to the libertine, the game will never seem worth the candle; while, should he persevere in the training so as to become an adept in the third and last degree, he will be no longer a libertine.

Third. There is a belief among some occultists that an earnest wish breathed at that time, when husband and wife are one, will not fail to be granted. This opens, it is said, the door to those who practice what is called "black magic", and enables them to work harm upon other human beings. What foundation there is for this belief as applied to the magicians I do not see. If it really be that a wish is granted then more readily than when the seeker is in any other mood, it is probably because the occultist who attains the second degree has to exercise such supreme self-control at that moment that he is complete master of his sub-consciousness, and if he has attained the third degree he is in rapport with Spirit throughout the universe, so that his desire is granted because he desires only what is in harmony with Good and Right. That a black magician should be able at such a moment to enter upon harmonious relations with the universe by breathing a curse seems to me very unlikely.

I am of the opinion that this belief is due to the mistaken idea that correct living and clear thinking are unnecessary to establish lines of accurate communication with the unseen world.

And, because occultists have usually assumed the nearness of a world of devils, rather than a world of angels, and because they have assumed that depravity and prejudice offer no bar to communication with unseen intelligences, whether good or evil, it was a most natural conclusion that it would be dangerous to entrust the secret of the third degree to a "black magician". But, so long as a man is a black magician, he will fail to enter upon the third degree.

This last degree is, I am firmly convinced, impossible, whether in earthly or Borderland wedlock, for either man or woman who does not live a pure life in self-control and aspiration to the Divine. And the occultist who seeks to attain to the third degree must first become a white magician.

Nevertheless, as I have said, the initiates in the third degree have guarded this secret most jealously, and apparently for the reasons I have assigned.

The first and second degree, however, seem to have been taught publicly in symbolic rites — such as for instance in that much misunderstood dance at the Columbian Exposition — the *Danse du Ventre*. It was noticeable that the oriental men, one and all, viewed the dance with serious and at times reverent gaze.

This fact was brought to my notice by two ladies (school teachers) who knew absolutely nothing of the Sex Worship symbolism of the dance, but who had concluded, simply from thoughtful observation, that there must be some religious and pure-minded motif back of it all. Nevertheless, most Americans and Europeans, whether men or women, failed to

penetrate beneath the surface of this markedly symbolic dance, owning to the occidental
habit of thought which sees naught but impurity in the most important and sacred function
of our nature. In Oriental countries, however,
despite their being "heathen", sex is looked on
as holy. In this connection, our phrase "Give
God the glory", takes on itself a vaster significance than is ever taught in our pulpits.

It is no wonder, then, the Oriental
occultists should have penetrated at an early
date to the underlying principles of marital
relations on the Borderland. From their life-
long habits of thought, they viewed sex as
simply and naturally as we should view the
circulation of our own blood — as a curious
phenomenon of absorbing personal interest.
With no false shame to overcome, they were
fitted to receive the higher truths concerning
this subject, whereas our Occidental mediums, for the most part, receive words of
impurity or are misled into a loose life. The
difference is due to the exact antipodal stand-
points of Occidental and Oriental psychics on
the subject of the holiness of sex.

I have said that the initiates of the third
degree seem to have made this the inner secret
of their mysteries, the world over, and, that
they have always jealously guarded this secret
from the masses. I am inclined to think that in
the beginning it may not have been so, but
that this jealous care may have been the result

of a bitter lesson learned of the unwisdom of throwing pearls before swine, not because the swine turn and rend one—for the earnest teacher of truth never gives his own danger a second thought—but because the swine are too apt to soil the pearls by trampling them in the mire.

If it be asked in amazement how this teaching of "Giving God the Glory" and sharing with Him the supreme joy of the marital relation could become so degraded by swinish human beings as to cause its teachers to withhold it in future from the masses, I answer:

By turning it into a commercial transaction with God.

The piggish, greedy man, learning by hearsay of the connubial bliss attending the Triune partnership with god, pressed eagerly forward with one thought uppermost: "I will pay God cash down for so much of my pleasure, and I mean to drive a close bargain with Him."

The voluptuary, seeking to enhance his physical sensations, likewise pressed forward, saying to himself in an outburst of generosity: "God shall receive from me every whit as much as He gives me."

The sentimental, but selfish, mystic, ever yearning for a new subjective experience, likewise pressed forward, thinking, "I shall get acquainted with God on intimate terms by dividing up my pleasure with Him."

Be not deceived; God is not mocked. Whatsoever a man soweth he shall reap.

And each of these types failed to get what they expected in pleasure, because it cannot be secured by any means but by love.

Now, these would-be initiates not only failed (to get so much physical pleasure for so much tithing paid over to Him), but they tempted by that very failure to enter upon what we may call (to put it euphemistically) not a new bargain.

The nervous system had been wrought to too high a pitch not to insist upon a purchase of some market—if not God's market, then in the Devil's. Hence, I fancy too often abnormal vices and abominations of ancient Sodom and Gomorrah of the Orient today and the Roman Empire when Christianity first turned its purifying (though salty) current through the Augean stables of latter-day Sex-Worship.

For this the initiates who held the whole truth, among other reasons no doubt, usually shrank from revealing even glimpses of it to any one who had not passed a long probation. According to the Talmud, the ancient Hebrews had three names to express the idea of God, the first of which was interdicted to the great number. Sages taught it once a week to their sons and their disciples. The second was at first taught to everybody. "But", said Maimonides, "when the number of the ungodly had increased, it was entrusted only to the most discreet among the priests, and they repeated it in a low tone to their brethren, while the people were receiving the benediction." The third name for god "contained", says Jacolliot, "the great secret of the universal soul, and stood for, if we may so express it, the highest degree of initiation." Regarding this last, Maimonides says: "It was only taught to a man of recognized discretion, of mature age, not addicted to anger or intemperance, a stranger to vanity, and gentle and pleasant to all with whom he was brought in contact."

"Whoever", says the Talmud, "has been made acquainted with this secret and vigilantly keeps it in a pure heart, may reckon upon the love of God and the favor of men; his name inspires respect; his knowledge is in no danger of being forgotten, and he is the heir of two worlds, that in which we live and the world to come."

All of which applies to the earthly partner of a celestial BRIDE or BRIDEGROOM, when the laws of correct living and clear thinking are obeyed. Those who know this secret and vigilantly keep it in a pure heart are indeed the heirs of both worlds, for they dwell upon the Borderland, harmoniously adapting their lives to both planes of existence and, being at one with God, they can each say, "If God be for me, who can be against me?" Nor is the reward for making a proper use of this Great

Secret confined to Borderland wedlock; its Kingdom may come on the earthly plane itself to worthy neophytes.

It was probably to keep the knowledge of this secret from the unworthy that the ancient mysteries of Isis and Eleusis were designed.

For this purpose, also, the sacred scriptures of all religions—not excepting the Hebrews and the Christians—seem to have introduced stories and aphorisms which should convey one meaning to an outsider, and quite another to an initiate.

> "Woe to the man who looks upon the law as a simple record of events expressed in ordinary language, for, if really that is all it contains, we can frame a law much more worthy of admiration. If we are to regard the ordinary meaning of the words, we need only turn to human laws and we shall often meet with a greater degree of elevation. Every word of the law contains a deep and sublime mystery."

—A. Franck's *"La Kabbale"*.

> "If the law were composed of words alone, such as the words of Esau, Hagar, Laban, and others, or those which were uttered by Balaam's ass or by Balaam himself, then why should it be called the law of truth, the perfect law, the faithful witness of God himself? Why should the sages esteem it as more valuable than gold or precious stones?
>
> "But every word contains a higher meaning; every text teaches something besides the events

*which it seems to describe. This superior law is the
more sacred, it is the real law."*

—Jewish Cabalists

The following occurs in the Book of the
Pitris (Pitris, according to Jacolliot, is the
name applied in India to the spirits of the
dead) with whom communication has long be
held, after the fashion of modern Spiritualism,
and with the same attendant phenomena:

*"The sacred scriptures ought not to be taken in
their apparent meaning, as in the case of ordinary
books. Of what use would it be to forbid their revelation to the profane if their secret meaning were
contained in the literal sense of the language usually
employed?*

*"As the soul is contained in the body,*

*"As the almond is hidden by the envelope,*

*"As the sun is veiled by clouds,*

*"As the garments hide the body from view,*

*"As the egg is contained in the shell,*

*"And as the germ rests within the interior of the
seed,*

*"So the sacred law has its body, its envelope, its
cloud, its garment, its shell, which hide it from the
knowledge of the world."*

*"You who, in your pride, would read the sacred
scriptures without the Guru's assistance, do you even
know by what letter of a word you ought to begin to
read them—do you know the secret of the combination by twos and threes—do you know when the final
letter becomes an initial and the initial becomes
final?"*

*"Woe to him who would penetrate the real
meaning of things before his head is white and he
needs a cane to guide his steps."*
— Quoted by Jacolliot, Oc. Sci. in India.

The closing paragraph becomes
significant, when we reflect upon the danger
which the initiates feared would accrue to
those still in the heyday of manhood's passions, if they proved unworthy of the Great
Secret. The expression "The secret of the
combination by twos and threes" has probably a double meaning here—the esoteric
meaning turning upon the two kinds of marital partnership known to the initiates;
husband and wife being the "combination by
*two*" (in the second degree), and husband,
wife and God, three in one, a sacred trinity in
unity, being the "combination by *three*" (in
the third and highest degree), and they who
have once realized the blessedness of this triune partnership will move heaven and earth
to make it renewable at will—so much
sweeter and more helpful in every way it is
than the mere "combination by two".

Now, because sex is distinctly emotional in
its manifestations, there is always a tendency,
with failure to reach the highest, to allow the
emotions to slump down, as it were, to a lower
level. Few natures are so supremely self-
controlled as to say, at a critical moment, "the
highest—or nothing. I will wait for that!" And

the types I have mentioned above as failure,
the piggish man, the voluptuary and the sentimental, selfish mystic—when, because of the
delicate balance required of the initiate who
would enter on the third degree, they slipped
off their pivot, fell quite outside the circle of
what is lawful, sure, and normal, to chaotic,
unlawful and horribly vile. From this, dates
much of the black magic. And this was the
controlling subjective influence which made
witchcraft a very real, objective terror to the
victims of the witches during the Middle
Ages. There is little doubt that many of the
witches did practice a sorcery of the most
diabolical type, a sorcery based upon the principles of hypnotic suggestion, and of the wilful
projection of the astral, or double; a sorcery
whose object was to cause evil, and which did
cause evil in many cases where the victims
were not protected from occult mischief-
working by living pure and upright lives; a
sorcery, finally, whose impelling motive was
due to insane hallucinations resulting in a very
large number of cases from having violated
the laws of right living in sex relations on the
Borderland. It is probable that many of these
witches passed the second degree, while few,
if any, gained the third—the inner degree
where aspiration in mingled purity and passion to union with God is chief factor. Some
of the attributes of a witch (we need not

enumerate them all; the literature of the subject is voluminous) were:

*That she sustained or was supposed to sustain occult sex relations with the Prince of the Powers of Air, Yclept the Devil;*

*That she received on some part of her body a devil's mark or stigma, which was his seal of authority over her and which seems to have been hypnotically rendered insensible to pain. There were men who did a business in discovering witches by pricking a suspected woman's body all over with a pin until they found some place insensible to the pain of the prick, when they would triumphantly announce this to be the "Devil's Mark";*

*That the Devil or one of his imps at times visited her in the guise of some animal—a dog, a cat, even a huge butterfly, to suck some part of her body, and that, whatever the part of her body chosen, it and no other spot was always resorted to by the impish creature thereafter. Sometimes witnesses testify to seeing these animal familiars, as in the case of a witch ill in bed who was being closely watched. The witness, who was on guard, testified with much detail of circumstance to having seen a huge "fly", like a miller, which buzzed in among the hair of the sick woman and after a while flew away, when the witch called to the witness to lift up her hair, that she might show a sore place on the scalp which, she said, was where the Devil, in the form of a fly, was wont to suck her.;*

*That she could work harm to people at a distance by what appears to have been hypnotic suggestion, and that she usually was wickedly and viciously inclined to do this at will.;*

*That she could appear in what seems to have been her double, or astral form, to her victims.*

Now, regarding this last, the extremely critical and level-headed Society for Psychical Research have collected some three thousand cases of apparitions of living doubles at the present day, all of them well attested by witnesses. Most of these apparitions (some of which were so like real flesh and blood as to be taken for the person himself), according to the Society's records, were spontaneous, only a few being deliberately self-induced—a fact which indicates that the projection of the double is probably a normal power and that it ought to be, therefore, not so very difficult for an illiterate old woman to acquire. A few apparitions of doubles seem to be due mostly to one of the following causes:

> *Violent shock, as a roadway accident, danger of drowning.*
>
> *A state of health indicative of approaching death, so that the astral form (is this the soul, the body of the immortal spirit?) seems already poised for flight.*
>
> *The moment of separation of soul and body, specially if caused by drowning, suffocation, contusion on the head, wounds received in battle, etc.*
>
> *Falling into a "brown study": gazing fixedly at an object in an abstracted way (self-hypnotization); listening abstractedly to a continuous and monotonous sound.*
>
> *Falling asleep with an earnest desire fixed in one's mind to visit such or such a person or place.*
>
> *Any of these may be induced accidentally and, so far as we know, without the conscious will of the ego.*

*Deliberately willing, under some of the above cir-*
*cumstances, to have one's double appear at such and*
*such a place. This act may or may not include—ac-*
*cording to the extent of the psychic's training—an*
*after-memory of the event.*

From the above it will be seen that the
apparition of the double, whether spontaneously or deliberately induced, seems to be
brought about by a sudden focusing of mental
force. I am inclined to think that some of the
surest vouchers for the material objective substantiality of the world beyond the grave will
be found among the phenomena attending the
appearance of the double; inasmuch as the
double, when most clearly manifesting, com-
ports itself like an earthly being, with earthly
necessities; and if this double be, as appears,
identical with the soul-body which quits our
mortal frame at death, we have only to collate
and compare instances of the earthly double,
and acquire the art of projecting our own double intelligently and without loss of memory
while in earth-life, and we shall know beyond
all doubts what its habits of thought, its
appetites and necessities are likely to be beyond the grave.

In the witchcraft days, what is called
"repercussion" was a common phenomenon.
That is, the witch who appeared in astral form
to her victims, if wounded with a knife, might
be afterwards found to have sustained a simi-

lar wound in her physical body. This carries
out the idea of the Theosophists and other
occultists, that thought has power over matter, and that our physical frame is in reality
moulded by the spirit and soul which inhabit
it. Col. Olcott gives an interesting account of
repercussion in his own case.

Instances are not wanting where the
earthly double has shown that its sex capacity
remains apparently unaffected by temporary
separation from the body. The following case,
though probably founded on the falsehood of
a clever woman (S.V. Feconditee), shows
with what serious respect the phenomenon of
the double was viewed some three hundred
and fifty years ago.

In the "Dictionaire Infernal" there is a
report of a trial before the Parliament of
Grenoble, in which the question was, whether
a certain infant could be declared legitimate
which was born after the husband had been
absent from his wife four years. The wife
asserted that the baby was the offspring of a
dream, in which she had a vivid idea that her
wandering spouse had returned to love and
duty. Midwives and physicians were con-
sulted, and reported on the subject. As a
result, the Parliament ordained that the infant
should be adjuged legitimate, and its mother
should be regarded as a true and honourable
wife. The judgment bears date 13th February,

1537. (Inmen's "Ancient Faiths and Modern", p. 265, footnote.)

The following incident was told to me by a gentleman who had heard it from the lips of one of the parties. For obvious reasons, I suppress even localities:

> "A gentleman who was intensely dark, of a Spanish type, was in love with a girl of the true blond type. They never married, but later on she married someone else and moved to another part of the country. One night this gentleman had a very vivid dream, in which he fancied himself to be her husband. So real seemed the experience that he could scarcely convince himself on waking that he had not actually just come from her presence. Several years later, he happened to be in that part of the country, and bethought himself of hunting up his former lady love. He found her husband to be a decided blonde, like herself. A little child, a decided brunette, ran up to him, exclaiming joyfully, "Papa, Papa!" "Well!" laughed the host, "I am glad that she has found someone to call `Papa', for she steadfastly refuses to recognize me as such." Whereupon the lady appropriately fainted. The visitor learned afterwards, by making inquiries of her, that she had had a dream similar to his at the same time, and just nine months previous to the birth of the child."

Was this a case of repercussion? Did his double meet her double (but not her physical self?) on the astral plane and was that thought-world more powerful in moulding her child than was her physical environment as a wife? Or was it merely a telepathic impression conveyed from his mind to hers with sufficient vividness to "mark" the child? I may here remark that I do not consider the theory that he was the physical father of the child, as it seems to me that that would be a violation of the natural laws of Borderland. Nevertheless, if he really was the physical father, the stories would only be in keeping with the stories of the giant progeny from angelic fathers, and the stories of women confined in high towers and yet becoming pregnant by a celestial visitor. In the case of Danae, her visitor materialized as a shower of gold—quite after the fashion of modern apparitions of spiritualistic seances where the spirits often materialize as floating masses of radiant mist. At recent seances, too, trained scientific observers have perceived the medium's double (I now speak of mediums who are not fraudulent and who are willing to submit to experimental tests) partially or wholly dissociated from the medium's physical self. Col. Olcott gives an interesting account of his double oozing through the walls of Mrs. Blavatsky's room on its way to the sitting-room to add three words to a MS. on which he had been busily writing just before retiring. Both the earthly double and the celestial spirit appear to possess this faculty of oozing through blank walls. May they not be one and the same? In that case, we see how easy it may be to confound spirit BRIDEGROOMS from the world beyond the grave (who cannot beget children on the Borderland because this would be a violation of natural laws), and astral doubles of earthly lovers who can stimulate the begetting of children upon the astral double of an earthly woman so vividly as to mark the child of her lawful husband and herself with the likeness of the astral lover.

At this point it may be objected that such information as I am here giving should not be spread broadcast, lest unscrupulous libertines take advantage of this power of projecting the double to get innocent girls into their power, since high towers and bolted doors appear to offer no barrier to the double's entrance. It is precisely for this reason that this information should be widely circulated, in order that these possibilities may be made known to the general public and guarded against. The present flood of Theosophic and other popular occult literature, as well as the published records of the S.P.R., have already placed the knowledge of this power within the reach of the libertine, if he chooses to avail himself of it.

When he can have this for the asking, it is high time that the general public know something of it also, as well as of the fact that correct living and clear thinking will always protect us from evil induced by occult means. It is an interesting question, however, as to whether children could really be begotten by a double upon a virgin or, as in the case tried before the Grenoble Parliament, upon a married woman whose husband is away.

I am inclined to think not, since the double is for the time being on a different plane of matter from the physical body; being, in fact, in the same world as it will be after death; so that it must obey the law of the Borderland quite as much as if it were an angelic BRIDEGROOM, which is to sow no seed, inasmuch as no harvest can be reaped therefrom. But in this case, what becomes of the scientific basis of such stories as Danae and other virgins who become the mothers of children by a Borderland lover — whether earthly double or heavenly angel? There is but one way, so far as I see, by which a Borderland BRIDEGROOM could beget a child by an earthly woman. The woman must live each moment in strict obedience to the laws of her earth-life and also of his heaven life. She must be capable of appreciating the intellectual thought of his advanced world. She must understand and live in accordance with the higher code of ethics current in his realm. She must neglect no earthly duty; she must be conversant with the intellectual thought-world of her earthly associates; she must not crush out a single instinct of her true nature, but properly use every physical appetite and passion to round out a symmetrical earthly life.

When emergencies arise on either the earthly plane or on the Borderland, she must never make a mistake, for to do so will cause the lines of communication to waver, and presently to part. In short, her life, judged not only by the highest earthly standard but by the more advanced standard in the world beyond the grave must be absolutely perfect, if she is to conceive, gestate for nine long months and give birth to a child begotten by a Borderland father; that is, she must be psychically on the same plane with him, and at the same time fulfill the laws of both planes, and without a single break. Only thus were the laws on the Borderland obeyed.

The Roman Catholic Church in its dogma of The Immaculate Conception claims perfection for the blessed Virgin Mary. In so doing, it shows its wisdom. Though I am by no means a Romanist, I emphatically say that from the occult standpoint the immaculate life of Mary for a long period prior to the Annunciation and until at least the birth of Jesus is the only foundation upon which the possiblity of the mysterious conception of Jesus as a Borderland child can rest. Having once attained this high plane, it is unlikely that she would ever descend to a lower plane afterward: so that, accurately speaking, the Roman Catholic doctrine of her immaculate life must

have been absolutely perfect on all points, or
she could not have conceived a child by a
HEAVENLY BRIDEGROOM (which is of God; for
God does not break his own laws.) Nor is it
likely that the HEAVENLY BRIDEGROOM would
break his laws in order to beget a child upon
an earthly woman provided that woman were
suitably trained for sometime for the occult
espousal, and provided that God has a tangible form, as He appeared to Moses to have
when he had Moses remain in the cleft of a
rock while He passed by. (Exodus XXXIII,
21, 21.) This is the strength of the one Catholic doctrine concerning Mary's stainlessness
in life; and from the Apocryphal Gospels, it
appears that Mary had had the advantage of
being brought up as an orphan in the temple
under the eyes of the priests. It was customary
for her to see and talk with angels and to
receive food from them before her espousal to
Joseph.

My own idea of it, however, is that such a
conception — if conception there were —
would require Mary's mentality to rise not
only to the standard of an angel but to the
omniscience and all pervading tenderness of
God, in order for her to be so thoroughly his
spouse on the Borderland as to conceive and
bear a child to him. On the other hand, it is
interesting to note in connection with this the
record in the Apocryphal Gospels as to the appearance of an angel visitor to Mary in the

guise of a handsome youth, and the opinion expressed to Joseph by the virgins left in charge of her during Joseph's absence, that it was the angel who had made her pregnant.

Perhaps, when we come into harmonious rapport with the mystical theory, popularized by the school of divine science and other mystics, that each one of us is a part of the universal mind, and that that mind may know all things in the universe, we might allow even this on the Borderland. However, the Roman Catholic Church has seemingly provided for the high standard of mentality required from a spouse of Divine Science on the Borderland by ascribing to Mary not only the name, but the attributes of "Mother of God".

In "The Perfect Way, or the Finding of Christ", written by Anna Kingsford and Edward Maitland, occurs a remark about "the notion, far from uncommon, that by abjuring the ordinary marriage relation, and devoting herself wholly to her astral associate, a woman may, in the most literal sense, become an immaculate mother of Christs". It is needless to add that the authors deprecate this, but their remarks show their total misapprehension of Borderland sex-relations, since it is only between husband and wife that those relations can exist objectively, all else is but subjective illusion. And, therefore, the command of Mary's HEAVENLY BRIDEGROOM that Joseph was not to approach her as a husband

until after the birth of the mysteriously begotten child would be strictly in keeping with
Borderland laws, monogamy, and not bigamy,
being the law of Borderland, because it is the
highest ideal of both worlds.

The mediaeval witch, as well as the Blessed
Virgin, had her chance of Borderland nuptials
on a high plane; but unlike Mary, she failed to
pass those ordeals which require correct living and clear thinking on the part of the
earthly psychic. In the first place, the witch
(poor woman) lived in days when the physiological relations of husband and wife occupied
a far lower place in popular estimation than it
did in the days of Mary and moreover, in the
Orient, Mary's home the relation of husband
and wife had then and still has a holiness on
its physiological side which is foreign to
European or American habits of thought.

When the peculiar psychical experiences
of the witch set in, therefore, she naturally
jumped to the conclusion that, first, they were
sinful; second that, being sinful, they were the
work of Satan. These assumptions were a departure from clear, unprejudiced thinking and
from that moment began her diabolical illusions, and she saw monsters, hobnobbed with
imps, was lashed by scorpions, etc. etc., to the
full extent of her willingness to receive these
illusions as objective realities.

The poor creatures, indeed, had not our
advantages in the perusal of records of

hypnotism and of the Society for Psychical Research, and would have been sadly puzzled to draw the line between subjective illusion and objective materialization. Nevertheless, her angel lover was with her when she thought him the Devil. He comforted her in her poverty and loneliness (many of these witches, remember, were old women, whose lives had been the bare, dreary lives of the terribly poor) and he promised her such influence among her neighbors as she longed for most. This was an ordeal, had she but known it, which, if passed successfully, would have brought her to a higher and sweeter pleasure. Some there were, here and there, who seem to have chosen the better part, and to have become "white witches", capable of clairvoyance, of healing human beings and cattle of strange diseases, forecasting the future and the like. But usually these poor old women had been so embittered against selfish or heedless neighbors that the influence they longed for most was to pay back their wrongs (real or supposed) with interest. Here again, they broke the occult law which calls for correct living on the part of the psychic, and trod the downward path of hatred and diabolism. In many cases, no doubt the psychical experiences of a witch started from this fierce desire to be revenged upon those who had slighted her. She probably began with some simple form of self-hypnotization imparted to her by a neighbor who had already acquired some proficiency in the art. Once she had accomplished this, the astral world lay open wide before her with all its illusions or all its realities, according to how she proved worthy of one or the other. Sometimes, no doubt, she struggled upward to benevolent thoughts and prayers for help in resisting temptation and was accordingly rewarded with true occult power and with union with her angelic mate who was both her husband and her guardian. That she thought him the Devil partially interfered with the physical strengthening and psychical happiness which that union brought; while he, on his part, kept steady watch over her infirmities, always ready to help the slightest impulse of her spirit to rise to higher things, seeing as only angels see, beneath that misshapen earthly body, the soul, the astral body, which, despite the temporary disfigurements caused by evil thoughts, is ever young and fair, and waiting patiently throughout her poor, stumbling, sinful life, as only a man who truly loves a wife can wait, for the time when she will live down her mistakes, and see as clearly as himself.

If it be objected that this occult wedlock with an angel whom she ignorantly mistook for a devil brought her to misfortune, I answer: *Not unless she broke the law of correct living by trying to turn her occult powers to base purposes, or failed to keep clear-headed.*

But in that case?

In that case, also, her guardian angel took her through the deep waters and along the rugged, toilsome mountain path for her evolution, that she might be made perfect through suffering. Are we not all convinced that that is what God means by putting us, who are not witches, in a world where each of us has to wrestle with adverse circumstances in bitterness of spirit? In our inmost being we recognize God's wisdom in our being taken through sorrows, temptations and conflicts, for thus only can we grow strong and rise to our full stature as made in His likeness.

And to the witch, Heaven was no less merciful than to us, in that it forced ordeals upon her which, when she passed them, brought her happiness, but which, when she failed to pass them, brought her suffering.

It is noticeable that most of the witches who came to grief, and who confessed to intercourse with the Devil, referred to certain ceremonies customary at each "Sabbath", although records of witchcraft point rather to subjective illusion of performing abominable rites than to actual practice of the same. For details, the reader may refer to almost any work on witchcraft.

He will there say that, with all the fuss made by the judges and persecutors about this intercourse with Satan, there was very little of real impurity, and what there was seems to have been entirely subjective—the illusion of an insane imagining. In short, the witch, as well as other BRIDES of angelic lovers, was evidently far from impure-minded by nature at the start, and this, too, in an age of vulgar expressions, coarse ideas and from which even the genius of Shakespeare did not escape without contamination.

Yet these women were mostly illiterate and miserably poor. It is probable that their poverty, however, had been their educator in ascetic deprivation and in bearing up under slights from more fortunate neighbors, and so had laid the foundations of that stern control of self which is absolutely necessary in the true occultist. That this feature—their feelings under slights received from neighbors—played an important part in their thoughts and consequently in their development is shown by the fact that many of their attempts (real or supposed) at bewitching date from an unkind refusal of a neighbor to give them a bowl of soup or an old shirt. Illtemper, then, morose broodings over wrongs, general sourness of spirit, were not the least important of the causes which turned those earthly partners of angelic BRIDEGROOMS into devil-haunted witches.

Another cause seems to have been their failure to think clearly and without prejudice.

Poor creatures! They were nearly all of them prejudiced (i.e., "pre-judgers") from beginning to end. They pre-judged angels to be the Devil; they pre-judged the monsters imagined by their own subconsciousness to be real; they pre-judged the wedlock into which they entered on the Borderland to be sinful; they pre-judged their mysterious visitor to be a tempter to lead them away from religion and the church they pre-judged him as requiring unhallowed rites—dimly remembered survivals from the ancient Sex Worship, too often on its vilest side; they pre-judged him as the means of ignoble satisfactions of their hatred and their animal desires. And thus they sank to diabolism.

There was yet another cause—not so much of evil as of illusions. This was the "Devil's Mark"—that special mark of his with which they supposed themselves stamped on some part of their bodies. With this, we may classify the spot at which the Devil or one of his imps was said to suck them, and also the peculiarity that their BRIDEGROOM in his marital relations chilled them as though with ice.

There are many phases of occult sensitiveness. The ear for the clairaudient, the eye for the clairvoyant, the easily swayed arm and hand for the writing medium, are the three physical organs through which communications usually reach us. But for the wife of a HEAVENLY BRIDEGROOM, the nerves of touch, it is evident, must be the chief focuses of occult sensitiveness. Now, in order that the delicate balance of nerve sensation be maintained, it is important that such a psychic distinguish readily between real touches and illusory touches, between objective realities impinging upon the ends of her nerves and hypnotic suggestions, either self-induced or induced by an outside intelligence; say by her spirit BRIDEGROOM. And not only must she learn to distinguish thus between real and unreal sensations, but she must also learn to resist all hypnotic suggestion to feel sensations which do not exist or which are unlawful. No psychic can be considered thoroughly self-controlled who has not acquired this power of resistance to hypnotic suggestion of unlawful touches or of unreal things as real. No psychic's testimony can be considered reliable so long as she fails to distinguish between genuine and illusory touches. So long as she is lacking in any of these essentials to the wife of a HEAVENLY BRIDEGROOM, just so long will her guardian persist in putting her though a course of training—a training which she must undergo until she passes her examination and is promoted into a higher class, there to take up still more advanced lessons in psychic discrimination and psychic self-control.

Now, the "Devil's Marks" and the "sucking" were both, so I hold, illusory sensations which the witch failed either to classify or to conquer, but to which she mistakenly succumbed. When the supposed Devil's mark showed non-sensitiveness to pin-pricks, it was probably a case of auto-suggestion—or, in the case of some, a hypnotic dulling to pain caused (oftentimes in mercy) by the angel guardian.

Of the same illusory character is that phenomenon which has so puzzled all the writers on witchcraft—the icy chilliness of the sperm. This experience is entirely subjective; because it is forbidden by Borderland laws to evoke a nervous energy for no definite result; and as a harvest in offspring on the Borderland cannot be produced, it is breaking Borderland laws to sow the seed.

The very fact that the Devil, who is supposed to be a deity of fire, seemed cold in the Borderland marital union, ought to have shown his earthly partner that it was an illusion. And the psychic who expects or thinks to enact a forbidden experience on the Borderland has only her own ignorance to thank for the illusion.

Incubi and Succubae, evil spirits who were supposed to force themselves as lovers upon both men and women, played an important part in witchcraft days. Deformed children were supposed to have sprung of such a union. Luther believed implicitly in this. Virtuous women seemed to be especially subject to the attacks of incubi, and this was looked on as attesting the cunning of Satan, who thus aimed at those noted for purity of life. It rarely, if ever, seems to have occurred to people in those days that a virtuous woman, reasonably clear-headed, is a being who is under especial angelic protection, and that when such a woman was persistently singled out by a spirit for lover-like attentions, it must have been owing to the favor of Heaven, and not to the malignity of devils. That these attentions became a great annoyance at last was only because the woman either broke the moral law in some way or became prejudiced against every such being as an emissary of Satan. In time, by the workings of the laws of Borderland, she who through natural curiosity and romantic sentiment at first hearkened to the angel lover and afterward, through the failure to live aright or think clearly, felt bound to reject him as a devil, became subject to hallucinations and also, in some cases, to annoying physical manifestations. Some picturesque stories have been told of such women, to whom the spirit lover has appeared in the guise of a handsome youth vainly wooing his earthly love night after night. The stories usually wind up with an account of fearful persecutions at the hands of the rejected lover who thus, by his malignity, reveals himself as the Devil. Sometimes the priest is appealed to but not always successfully. The Roman Catholic church has a regular rite to exorcise demons and is probably successful with the psychic through hypnotic suggestion. But in the case of a spirit lover who has once been received (whether as husband or only communicating spirit), it would seem as though his hypnotic suggestions often outweighed that of the priest. But I am inclined to think that the very lingering of these subjective experiences indicates that her psychic hallucinations were often not only due to hypnotic suggestions by her spirit lover, but also the result recorded in her subliminal consciousness of a veridical phenomenon which she at first encouraged, whether through harmless curiosity or through the romantic and tender sentiment of a pure heart, or through the grosser impulses arising from a luxuriant and untrained imagination, it matters not. When her season of ordeals set in and she was obliged to distinguish between the illusory and the real, in order to maintain communication with her interesting visitor, she either grew alarmed at the phenomena of the ordeals or rashly assumed the whole thing to be diabolical. From this time on, it were indeed strange if she should fail to see subjectively what she expected—i.e., the Devil. All in vain now was it for her to exclaim in terror or indignation: "I will have nothing to do with you!" Her angelic lover had indeed ceased to communicate; but her subconsciousness had not ceased to vibrate along the lines of psychical illusion; and, unless she possessed great self-control and had her sub-conscious nature well in hand, time and time only could work a cure, unless, indeed, she should implicitly submit her inner self to the priest or to some other earthly human being as her hypnotizer, in which case it was a change from the hypnotic control of a clear-seeing angel to that of a more or less blind, fallible man of earth who may or may not take undue advantage of the power placed in his hands over her mainsprings of action. When one—

Considers that every nun who enters a convent is pledged to a mystic union with a HEAVENLY BRIDEGROOM, denominated Christ;

That the union more often than the public is aware becomes so objectively real that the confessor feels obliged to term it "Congressus cum daemonis";

That ignorance on the nun's part of Borderland laws will render her experiences fantastic or diabolical;

That her deliverance from these experiences may be secured by a change in hypnotizer, from an unseen angel to a visible earthly priest—

—we see that a power resides with confessors to mould the minds of the nuns to carry out this hypnotic suggestion for the glory of the church. For the person who has been hypnotized by spirits and who has not acquired the power of resisting hypnotic suggestion will more readily yield to an earthly hypnotizer. That the angelic lover should force himself upon her as an incubus against her will is contrary to Borderland laws; for in the world beyond the Borderland (the world beyond the grave) it is reckoned a sin for a woman to have aught to do with a husband or lover save for love's sake, and hence the idea that a woman may be forced into a marital union on the Borderland is totally incorrect, inasmuch as the highest standards of social and ethical duty in both worlds must be lived up to by the two who meet upon the borders of the two worlds. Rationalists have tried to explain the spirit BRIDE and spirit BRIDEGROOM as a nightmare arising from a plethoric condition of the body—an explanation which has force only when the spirit is an incubus and not a succubus, and when the earthly psychic (man or woman) is asleep or dozing. But the clearest and most convincing manifestations of the objectivity of the HEAVENLY BRIDEGROOM always come when the psychic is most clear-headed. It seems, indeed, that it is not even in a trance but only when the psychic is wide awake that the marital union takes place objectively. And this, I think, will be found to be the case with the witches. When

their union with the supposed Devil was
based on the faithful tender love of one
woman for one man and its reciprocity, in accordance with high moral standards, then was
the union objective and natural. The gross
rites of the Witches' Sabbaths, with their ab-
normalities and absurdities, were evidently
the illusions of an insane imagination in great
part—although it is also doubtless true that,
as Professor Wilder says, "There is little reason to doubt that these `Witches' Sabbaths'
were formerly celebrated and that they were,
in some modified form, a continuation of the
outlawed worship of the Roman Empire."

Early in the 17th Century, a light dawned
upon the horizon of these illusions and
diableries. That light was the manifesto of a
secret society of mystics called the
Rosicrucians or followers of the Rosie Cross.
In 1605, the sect became known; in 1623 it
placarded Paris with mysterious announce-
ments; but it professed to have existed long
before. Who its members were, whether the
society really existed, or whether the whole
affair was a joke on the mystics, are questions
which today remain still unsettled. But,
whether a reality or a myth, the Rosicrucians
were a factor in the literature and mysticism
of their time, and a secret society of the same
name still exists. They dealt a powerful blow
at the superstition which assumed the spirit

BRIDEGROOM and the spirit BRIDE to be diabolical.

"They discarded forever all the old tales of sorcery and witchcraft and communion with the devil. They said there were no such horrid, unnatural and disgusting beings as the incubi and succubi and the innumerable grotesque imps that men had believed in for so many ages. Man was not surrounded with enemies like these, but with myriads of beautiful and beneficent beings, etc.—all anxious to do him services. The sylphs of the air, the undines of the water, the gnomes of the Earth, and the salamanders of the fire were men's friends, and desired nothing so much as that men should purge themselves of all uncleanness, and thus be enabled to see and converse with them. They possessed great power, and were unrestrained by the barriers of space or the obstructions of matter. But man was in one respect their superior. He had an immortal soul, and they had not. They might, however, become sharers in man's immortality if they could inspire one of that race with the passion of towards them. Hence it was the constant endeavor of the female spirits to captivate the admiration of men, and of the male gnomes, sylphs, salamanders and undines to be beloved by a woman. The object of this passion, in returning their love, imparted a portion of the celestial fire, the soul; and from that time forth the beloved became equals to the lover, and both when their allotted course was run entered together into the mansions of felicity. These spirits, they said, watched constantly over mankind by night and day. Dreams, omens, and presentiments were all their work, and the means by which they gave warning of the approach of danger. But though so well inclined to befriend man for their own sake, the want of a soul rendered them at times capricious and revengeful; they took offence at slight causes, and heaped *injuries instead of benefits on the heads of those who extinguished the light of reason that was in them by gluttony, debauchery, and other appetites of the body."*

— "Mackay's Popular Delusions. Mysteries of the Rosie Cross", by A. Reader, Orange Street, Red Lion Square, London, 1891.

There is a book called "Sub Mundanes", which in a vein of delicate humor deals with this belief of the Rosicrucians. It purports to be written by an acquaintance of one Count of Gabalis. It was published by the Abbot de Villars, nephew of Montfaucon, in 1670.

Sub Mundanes refers to stories told of the Gothic Kings being born from a bear, and a princess of Pegusians being born from a dog and a woman; of a Portuguese woman, who was exposed on a deserted island, having children by a large monkey. The author goes on to say that the sylphs of the Rosicrucians, seeing that they are taken for demons when they appear, in order to diminish aversion take the form of these animals, and accommodate themselves thus to the whimsical weakness of women, who would be horrified at the sight of a handsome sylph, but less so at a dog or monkey.

Sub Mundanes tells a story of a hard-hearted Spanish beauty who repulsed a Castillian gentleman so effectually that he left her and set off to travel to forget her; a sylph fell in love with her, took the shape of her absent lover, wooed her persistently and won her. A son was born; and when she was again pregnant, the earthly lover returned to Seville, quite cured of his passion, and hastened to call on her, saying he should now displease her no longer, as he had ceased to lover her. Result: a scene, tears, reproaches on the part of the young woman; parents come in and the whole matter is brought to light. The writer continues:

*"And what part played the Airy-Lover (interrupted I) all this while? I see well enough (answered the Count) that you are displeased that he should forsake his mistress, leaving her to the Rigour of her parents and to the Fury of the Inquisitors. But he had reason to complain of her: she was not devout enough; for when these gentlemen immortalize themselves they work seriously, and live very holily; that they lose not the right which they came to acquire of Sovereign good. So they would have the person to whom they are allied live with exemplary innocence."*

Sub Mundanes also tells of a young Lord of Bavaria who was not to be comforted for the death of his wife, whereupon a Sylph took her shape and appeared to him. The same story, as told elsewhere, however, stated that it was his own wife who returned from beyond the grave. They lived together many years, and had children. But "he swore, and spoke lewd, uncivil words". She reproved him vainly, and at last "she vanished one day from him, and left him nothing but her Clothes, and the Repentance of his not having followed her Holy Counsels."

These two stories show what stress is laid by the spirit lover upon the necessity for the earthly psychic to keep the moral law.

Another story, unreal and fantastic as is the catastrophe, shows that bigamy is not condoned on the Borderland, and that no man can serve two mistresses without punishment, when one of the earthly partners of one of these nymphs is his Borderland spouse. It appears that he

> "—was so dishonest a Man as to fall in Love with a Woman; but as he Dined with his new Mistress, and certain of his Friends, there was seen in the Air the Loveliest Creature of the World; which was the invisible Lover, that had a mind to let herself be seen by the Friends of her unfaithful Gallant; that they might Judge how little reason he could have to prefer a Woman before her. After which the enraged nymph struck him dead immediately."

> —Sub Mundanes.

But popular prejudice regarding the reality of witchcraft died hard. The Rosicrucians were charged with doing as did the witches — protecting their astral forms for selfish and lawless purposes. It was believed by the populace, and by many others whose education should have taught them better, that gentle maidens who went to bed alone often awoke in the night and found men of shape more beautiful than the Grecian Apollo, who immediately became invisible when an alarm was raised.

But this seems rather unlikely, when we carefully consider the following pronunciamento with which they placarded Paris;

> *"We, the deputies of the principal College of the brethren of the Rosecross have taken our abode, visible and invisible, in this city by the grace of the Most High towards whom are turned the hearts of the just. We shew and teach without books or signs, and speak all sort of languages in the countries where we dwell, to draw mankind, our fellows, from error and from death."*

Moreover, the Rosicrucians maintained most positively that the very first vow they took was one of chastity, and that any of them violating that oath would be deprived at once of all the advantages he possessed, and be subject to hunger, thirst, sorrow, disease and death like other men. Witchcraft and sorcery they also "most warmly repudiated". (Mysteries of the Rosie Cross, by A. Reader.)

And the editor of "Sub Mundanes", in a footnote, refers to the Rosicrucian marriage with the elementary or Spirit-life, esteemed a duty by the sages and cultivated with fasting, watching, prayer and contemplation and acquiring thereby that condition of spiritual repose, in which only inspired visions occurred.

Why did these mystics call themselves "Rosicrucian"? Some writers have attempted to derive the name from two words meaning "dew" and "cross"; but the usual interpretation is "followers of the Rosy Cross" —a cross with a rose being used as the society's symbol. Some derive the word from the name Christian Rosenkreutz, the reputed founder of the society; but in view of the fact that it is uncertain that he ever lived, and that the stories told about the opening of his tomb 120 years after his death have a decidedly mystical flavor one may be pardoned for considering this personage a myth, invented as a convenient explanation to outsiders to throw them off the track of the real meaning of the society's name.

Now, the cross is an old, old religious symbol of the union of man and woman the world over and dates from an unknown antiquity. The rose is a well-known symbol of love under its most ardent form. We have already seen that the Mexican Virgin, Sochiquetzal, was presented by heavenly messenger with a rose when the annunciation was made that she should bear a mysteriously begotten son; that her name means the "lifting up of roses"; and that this event marks the commencement of an epoch called "the age of Roses". We have seen that the Mexican Eve sinned by plucking roses which elsewhere are called, apparently, "the fruit of the tree". We have seen that quite on the other side of the world among the Mohammedans is found a tradition that Christ was conceived by the smelling of a rose, and there is an Eastern legend that the burning bush in which the angel of the Lord appeared to Moses—a bush which burned without being consumed—was a rose bush. May not these roses be symbolically one and the same with the rose upon the Rosicrucian cross? If so, remembering the Rosicrucian teachings about the duty of chastity, the joy of nuptials with a being from the unseen world, and the obligation to enter upon that heavenly marriage with "fasting, watching, prayer and contemplation", we may well believe that they had learned the inner mystery of aspiring through passion to communion with God and of placing the rose of Divine Love upon the cross of marriage union in Borderland wedlock.

Also in a book entitled "In the Pronaos of the Temple of Wisdom", by Franz Hartmann, occurs a list of Rosicrucian symbols followed by the significant remark: "He who can see the meaning of all these allegories has his eyes open."

Many of these symbols are evidently phallic, and yield easily to the interpretation that they are symbols in the training of the occultist in the three degrees to which I have already referred.

But, despite the good work done by the Rosicrucians in lifting Borderland wedlock to a higher plane in the estimation of the public, it was not all plain sailing yet. The Church — that conservator alike of the useful and the useless things of the past — clung to the old belief of witchcraft days. When one of her mystics — either nun or priest — became thus espoused, the Church seems to have steered a middle course between the old and the new. Usually she termed such experiences "Congressus cum daemone", and bent her powers to exorcizing the evil one. But occasionally, as in the case of St. Teresa, the nun was a clear-headed woman of known integrity and purity "Congressus cum daemonibus" was out of the question where such a woman was one of the parties to the union in these instances. By what one can only call an inspiration from on high the Church promptly decided that the "congressus" was not diabolical, but heaven sent.

And, since the nun was the professed "BRIDE of Christ"; what more natural than that her experience should be viewed as a mystical union with this Divine BRIDEGROOM? In this, the Church acted according to her light, and I think it must be admitted she did fairly well, considering the ignorance and prejudice of the times.

It is noteworthy, however, that in St. Teresa's case her confessor, after having her write out a detailed account of her experience, ordered her to burn a great part of it. Was it because the objectivity of her experiences did not harmonize very well with the mystical idea of "espousal to Christ"?

Latin scholars will notice that the laws of Latin syntax require a word to be supplied in translating this phrase—a general term, such as the word "something", or "that which belongs to". As this grammatical construction was used by a very learned Roman Catholic priest when discussing the matter with me, I cannot suppose it to be a slip of the tongue, as I should have supposed, had the speaker been less of a scholar. This construction, however, instead of obscuring, really sets forth the matter with clearer resemblance to the psychic's useful physiological experience, as will be seen by comparing it with the legends I have referred to regarding the finding of the body of Osiris by Isis. Only by comparing this Latin expression with the legends and their application will this phrase be properly understood.

Where the earthly partner in these unions was a woman, and a nun at that, pledged to unfaltering obedience to her official superiors, it was probably an easy matter for her

confessor to lump all her experiences—
veridical as well as illusory—under one head-
ing, that of subjective. A virgin is usually, by
reason of her environment as a woman, so ignorant of the physiology of marriage that it is
difficult for her as a psychic to distinguish
what is real from what is unreal until she has
been a Borderland wife for some time. But for
the priest to whom the blessed experience of
Borderland wedlock came in all its fullness, a
different course of treatment must have been
necessary, since, being a man, with the oppor-
tunities of knowledge open to a man, and to a
priestly confessor of sinful men and women,
he could not be hoodwinked by his superior
into taking for subjective illusions these experiences which were distinctively objective.
The records of witchcraft contain accounts of
priests who were burned at the stake for a
union of this sort extending over forty and
fifty years, with a spirit assumed to be the
Devil in the form of a woman.

Pope Gregory VII, who is known as
Hildebrand, that pope who strove so persistently to purge the priesthood of simony and
unchastity and to emancipate the Church
from interference by the temporal power, was
said to have a familiar spirit with whom he
maintained such a union.

But what is done with priests nowadays
who enter upon Borderland wedlock is not, so
far as I can learn, revealed to the general

public. From a French physician, however, I learned of a custom among the Continental priests concerning their sleeping arrangements which suggests that more allowance is made nowadays than formerly for those whom Heaven has thus singled out, and that the Church bows to the will of Heaven in this matter, and lays no blame upon the priest.

Theophile Gautier has written a novelette called Clarimonde, which recounts the love of a beautiful vampire woman for a priest. She comes to him each night and they mount and gallop away to her palace, whence he returns at daybreak for his priesthood duties. The author represents the priest as struggling between his duties as a priest and what he considers the allurements of sin; and in consonance with the idea that punishment is visited upon the sinner, Gautier reveals her as a vampire sucking the blood of her lover while he sleeps.

It would seem as though the author was catering to the popular superstition that it was sinful, specially for a priest of God, to enjoy sensuous love. But if anyone in the world is entitled to the joys of true Borderland wedlock, it is surely a priest who has kept his vows of asceticism, and who is really pure-minded. If anyone in the world needs it, it is surely the priest who is supposed to stand midway as a bridge-builder between earthly sinners and celestial beings of the unseen world beyond the grave, since it is pretty generally acknowledged that a well-ordered sex life is necessary to the development of a symmetrical character. For, what mean the words "holy" and "holiness"? They mean "whole-ly", "wholeness". The man or woman who expects to be indeed "holy" must be "whole" i.e., symmetrical. In Old Testament times, Jehovah forbade any priest who was a eunuch to minister before Him, thus recognizing the importance of sex in the perfect man.

The Rev. Arthur Devine, Passionist, in a book entitled "Convent Life, or the Duties of Sisters Dedicated in Religion to the Service of God", 1889—a book which, the title-page shows, is "intended chiefly for superiors and confessors"—takes up the subject of nuns who are subject to visions and supernatural revelations. Considering the question as to whether such experiences are true visions or the results of deception and error, he mentions as one test the consideration of "Whether it (the revelation) contains anything false, because in this case it cannot proceed from the spirit of truth: Therefore, it is necessary to consider whether it is confirmable to Scripture, to faith and morals, to theology and to the doctrine and traditions of the Church. Are they (these communications) accompanied by the cross and by mortification, and do they tend to the manifestation of the faith and the utility of the Church?" From which it will be seen that a HEAVENLY BRIDEGROOM who is not a good Catholic has every prospect of being classed as demoniacal, if he happens to fall in love with a nun and to tell her that he is not of the same religious belief as herself. This is a case where religious prejudice furnishes the standard by which to test the communication. Andrew Lang, speaking of some table-turning experiments by the Swiss investigator M. de Gasparin, remarks: "It would seem that the Roman Catholic Church, upon any subject when dealing with occult phenomena, is certain to bring about occurrences of a fantastic, misleading or diabolical character.

The "spiritus percutiens", "rapping spirit" (?), conjured away by old Catholic formulae at the benediction of churches, was brought forward by some of M. de Gasparin's critics. As *his* tables did not rap, he had nothing to do with the "spiritus percutiens". This proves, however, that the Roman Church was acquainted with raps, and explained them by spiritualistic hypothesis.

> *"A learned priest has kindly looked for the alleged* spiritus percutines *in dedicatory and other ecclesiastical formulae. He only finds it in benedictions of bridal chambers, and thinks it refers to the slaying spirit in the Book of Tobit."*
> —Andrew Lang, "Cock Lane and Common Sense", pp. 316-317.

The "slaying spirit" in the Book of Tobit, it will be remembered, was a so-called evil spirit who was in love with Sara and who objected to her marrying, and who slew seven successive earthly aspirants to her hand on the bridal night of each. He is always referred to as an instance of the incubus. But let us not forget that so-called incubi are angels, and are never evil; since in order to hold communication with the beloved earthly person they, as well as the psychic, are obliged to live correctly and think clearly. And what is evil on the Borderland is always subjective and never objective.

And the number seven, too, in regard to the husbands of a virgin who already has a spouse has a suspiciously mythical, folklorish look.

That the Roman Catholic Church should take account of such a spirit in the benedictions of bridal chambers shows that it has had good reason to suspect the visits of incubi to the virgins of its laity, as well as to the virgins of its nunneries. Indeed, Tylor in his "Primitive Culture" tells us that the frequency of incubi and succabae "is set forth in the Bull of Pope Innocent VIII, in 1484, as an accepted accusation against many persons of both sexes, forgetful of their own salvations, and falling away from the Catholic faith."

The following, which I take from *"Sub Mundanes"*, refers to one of the most noted instances in convent life of an incubus who was objectively as well as subjectively the spouse of a nun.

> *"A little Gnome got into the affections of the famous Magdalen of the Cross, Abbess of a Monastery at Cordova in Spain; she made him Happy when she was but twelve years old; and they continued their 'Amours Libres' for the space of thirty years until an ignorant Director persuaded Magdalen that her Lover was a Fiend; and forced her to demand absolution of Pope Paul III. Yet it was impossible that this could be a Demon; for all Europe knew, and Cassidorus Reniris has made known to all Posterity, the great miracles which daily were wrought in Favor of this Holy Woman; which certainly had never come to pass, if her "Amours Libres" with the Gnome had fallen so Diabolick as the Venerable Director imagined."*

Another account, however, informs us that the abbess was accused by her nuns of magic — "a very convenient accusation in those days when a superior was at all troublesome" — and that she very cleverly anticipated them by going to the Pope to confess all and throw herself on his mercy. Inasmuch as he granted her absolution, one cannot help wondering if he did not read between the lines of this confession the occult truth and recognize her as a lawful Borderland spouse.

I have already referred to the Song of Solomon as being interpreted by Christian commentators, and said to be a poetical statement of the rapturous union between Christ and his BRIDE, the Church. A sidelight is thrown upon the interpretation by a note in Kitto's illustrated Bible, which quotes Lane (Modern Egyptians) as saying that the odes sung by Mohammedans at religious festivals were of a similar nature when the Song of Solomon, generally alluding to the Prophet as the object of love and praise. In the small collection of poems sung at Zikrs, it appears, is one ending with these lines:

> "The phantom of thy form visited me in my slumber; I said: `O phantom of slumber! who sent thee?'
>
> occurrences of a fantastic, misleading or diabolical character...
>
> He said: `He sent me whom thou Knowest:
> He whose love occupies thee.
>
> The beloved of my heart visited me in the darkness of night.
>
> I stood to show him honor, until he sat down.
> I said, `O thou, my petition and all my desire!
> Hast thou come at midnight, and not feared the watchmen?'
>
> He said to me, `I feared; but, however, love
> Had taken from me my soul and my breath.'"

Finding that songs of this description are exceedingly numerous, and almost the only poems sung at Zikrs; that they are composed for that purpose and intended only to have a spiritual sense (though certainly not understood in that sense by the generality of the vulgar), I cannot entertain any doubt as to the design of "Solomon's Song."

This religious mysticism finds a modern echo in a little publication recently issued by the Adi Brahma Samaj of Calcutta, as the first step in a new propaganda. It is entitled "The Religion of Love". In its pages occur the words:

*"Though these terms, Father, Mother, Friend, Husband of the soul, are allegorical, they very aptly express our sweet relationship with God, and we have every right to use them. Among these allegorical designations the Husband of the Soul is the best."*

Zanchius wrote an "Excellent Traite du Mariage Spirituel Entre Jesus Christ et son Eglise", in which he drew a close parallel between earthly wedlock and the spiritual and divine marriage of Christ with the Church Universal. Among other things he laid stress on that scriptural saying of earthly husband and wife, that the twain shall become one flesh; and he said that, according to Scripture, it was neither God the Father nor God the

Spirit who is Spouse of the Church, but the Son, who was made of like nature with ourselves — like in all things to us, but without sin. He added:

> "His soul does not pervade all space, because it went out of his body when he died and consequently was not in all places, since going out of the body it did not remain therein, afterwards being returned to the body and never was and never will be (any more than the body) in all places.
>
> "In this spiritual marriage, all the person of each faithful one—that is to say, the body and the soul—is conjoined with all the person of Jesus Christ, and is made one flesh and one person with him."

As to the method by which this combined fleshly and spiritual union of Christian with his Christ can take place, Zanchius seemed to think that the Eucharist in which one partakes of the body and blood of Christ is the sole appointed means.

Now, the Eucharist, or the use of bread and wine in a sacred rite, was an old Pagan custom bound up with the idea of entering into blood brotherhood, of which Jesus made use to emphasize his own brotherhood with his disciples. The ceremony of the Eucharist was found in Peru when the Jesuits first landed. In fact, it is a very, very ancient rite existing in widely separated countries. The

Christian writer, Arnobius, rebukes in cutting terms the Pagan mock modesty which blushed at the mere mention of "bread and wine" —a matter which indicates some folklore connection between the Eucharist and sex; and if so, then between the Eucharist and the ancient mysteries of phallicism. Inasmuch as by far the greater part of all that was pure and holy in Phallicism is bound up with Borderland wedlock, it is possible that the eucharist may have esoterically a wider significance than either Arnobius or Zanchius was aware.

Modern believers in the union with Christ have taken a less mystical and more practical view of it than did Zanchius. Mrs. M. Baxter of the well-known institution for Divine Healing, Bethleham, London, has issued a little pamphlet on that text of 1st Corinthians VI. 13. "The body for the Lord, and the Lord for the body." In it she says:

> "One of the most successful devices of Satan has been his attempt to divorce our bodies from our souls in their relation to God. Your soul is the Lord's, of course, but your body is your own. You must serve the Lord with your soul, but enjoy yourself with your body! Such is his counsel to those whose tendency is gross and carnal, such as easily become drunkards, fornicators, or prostitutes, and form the large class of fallen men and fallen women in our midst. To another class he comes and says,

`You are religious; but it is your soul with which
you can serve God; all you can do with your body
is to punish it, and destroy it by slow degree.' Many
look upon this as religious heroism; but it is as
much a lie to the truth of God as is the grosser
misuse of the body for lust or appetite. God comes
with his glorious claim, `the body is for the Lord,
and the Lord for the body."

"Under the Divine Touch", a pamphlet
written by Chester E. Pond of Philadelphia,
contains the following recorded experiences,
which, mystical as they may be considered
from one standpoint, are singularly suggestive
of the earlier experiences of the psychic who
has entered on Borderland wedlock, but who
has not yet learned to distinguish between
subjective and objective touches—that is,
between a touch which is material, tangible,
real, and one that is only a hypnotic suggestion made by the Borderland spouse.

For the last eleven months, my whole being has been open more or less to the joys,
delights and peculiar sensations of heaven.
Recently the Lord has been giving me his
choicest foretastes of heavenly blessedness
just before I rise in the morning. During
these eleven months I have been daily and
almost hourly conscious of His positive and
holy touch in some part of my natural body.
But during these recent morning experiences
His touch has been more sweet and more
powerful than usual. These heavenly experi-

ences, when viewed from a human standpoint, seem remarkable. But when viewed from a heavenly standpoint, they seem perfectly natural. They have come to me very gradually. In every way they have been orderly and helpful. They seem just what might be expected to come to any devout Christian. For the Lord is no respecter of persons. In considering these experiences it should be borne in mind that Jehovah Jesus is in every way infinite, that He never makes two things just alike in the natural world, and that He never acts twice alike in the spiritual world. Hence, as might be expected, He touches my `natural body' through my `spiritual body' in an infinite variety of ways, and with infinite sweetness. But for convenience I will classify and say that He touches me, *first*, directly or immediately. *Secondly*, He touches me through the medium or ministration of angels and, *thirdly*, through the medium of His Written Word.

To my distinct consciousness the spirit of the Lord is that living divine or divine substance which constantly proceeds from His divine person, somewhat in the same way and manner that rays of light and heat are continually proceeding from our natural sun.

It is written that `God is love' and that `God is light', or truth. From this we learn that love and truth constitute the divine essence. And in the ordinary use of language, heat corresponds to love and light to truth. We call a loving person warm-hearted, and an educated person enlightened. Jesus Him-

self taught spiritual truths by natural
symbols.

The Lord, in His mercy, tempers the
inflowing of His spirit to our different states
of receptivity. If He had poured His divine
love and truth into my soul and body one year
ago, with the same degree of heat and power
that He does now, I believe I should have
been consumed.

My experiences are endless in variety. At
times, when love seems to predominate over
truth, the divine proceeding that streams
forth upon me appears to my spiritual vision
like the golden beams of autumn sunset, but
when truth predominates over love, they appear like streams of white light reflected from
burnished silver.

At times I am consciously alone with the
Lord. At other times I am consciously in the
presence of angels. Since these touches of the
Lord are infinite in variety, I can never tell
one minute what will occur the next. As I
now sit writing I am so literally full that
every particle of flesh in my body feels as if
it were alive and moving. This extreme fulness in the daytime does not occur every day.
It will probably not continue more than eight
or ten hours. While I am busy it is not exces-
sively delightful. But if I were to lean back in
my chair, or to go and lie down, I should soon
be completely deluged with floods of heavenly glory, and be `lost in wonder, love and
praise.' The movings of the spirit are usually
undulatory. When I am still, and sometimes
when at work, they come like waves of liquid
sweetness, and roll over me and through me

in every conceivable direction, and with all conceivable variety.

Occasionally at night the Lord touches me all over alike for a few seconds. At such times I seem to be literally resting *in* and *on* the Divine. Sometimes He touches only a few fibres in some very small muscle, and through these He fills and thrills my whole being with unutterable divine glory. At times His holy touch is very delicate, tender and meltingly sweet. At other times He touches me with a power that moves the very foundations of my being, and that seems almost startling. Sometimes He moves very slowly, at other times so rapidly that it seems as if the next wave of glory would loosen my `spiritual body' from its present moorings in the `natural body'.

A few mornings ago while lying in bed under a divine influx that filled me with divine love and sweetness to the very utmost extent of my present capacity, I could but exclaim,

'O Jesus, my dear heavenly Father! Thou alone art infinitely wise and infinitely holy! In Thy presence I am nothing, I am nothing! Before Thee I know nothing, I know nothing. These sweet touches of Thy spirit, these indescribable sensations, these angelic delights, these ineffable thrills of divine glory I cannot understand! I can now understand them no better than if I were a new-born infant lying at Thy feet! Such knowledge is too wonderful for me; it is high, I cannot attain unto it! Dear heavenly Father, I can no more understand how each divine touch can fill me with such holy sweetness and with such transports of joy than I can understand how Thou canst create a world!

*'O Thou Eternal Word, by whom the worlds were framed! I can no more comprehend Thy present movings within my own little body than I could have comprehended the ancient movings of Thy spirit upon the face of the great deep if I had been present when Thou didst say, `Let there be light, and there was light'.*

Through the loving touch and conscious presence of an angel, be it a man or a woman, the Lord can fill me with celestial delights and sensations that are similar and almost equal to those produced by the direct inflowing of His own holy spirit. The difference between the two is easily discernible, but not easily described. Both are immeasurably superior to any soul or bodily delight we ever experience in the ordinary planes of Christian life. As near as I can describe it, the difference between the two is this: When waves of glory are produced by the direct touch of the Divine Spirit they seem to have, as it were, a golden tinge, a delicate crest of holy sweetness, which does no accompany those produced through the touch of an angel.

The angels are so thoroughly honest, so perfectly free from all false modesty and pretended humility, and are so free from all formality and human ceremonies, that the presence of an angel is always elevating and refreshing.

The Lord touches me consciously now through the medium of His Written Word... When I read the Scriptures my whole `spiritual body' can feel the touch and power of the Living Divine that flows through its words and sentences, just as plainly and unmistakably as my natural body can feel the touch and force of the wind.

And at times the `Spirit of Truth' flows all through me, and all over me, so forcibly that I feel as if I were literally `in the Truth'. At these times the Eternal Word shines through the Written Word with such illuminating power that various human theories and speculations are scattered to the four winds. And under such illumination `it is given to know the mysteries of the Kingdom of God'... I can learn more in one hour under such practical tuition than I ever learned in a whole year at Yale Theological Seminary.

In religion, theories have their uses, but the school of experience is the only school that can be relied upon for instruction in the mysteries and deep things of God. It often seems to me as if the Christian world, ministers included, were looking more to their creeds, and to one another, for their theology, than to the Word and the Spirit.

Before anyone can become personally acquainted with the Lord, and with the true meaning of His written Word, he must necessarily forsake every known sin and he must know what it means to live up to every known requirement and privilege of the Gospel. He must also ask for and receive a tender conscience, an enlightened reason, and a sanctified common sense. Then he will no long be afraid to use his own reason and his own good sense. I have recently received from the Lord, as I believe, the following unsectarian motto: "Love everybody, learn of everybody, and follow nobody but the Lord Jesus Christ.

To obtain and retain constant Divine guidance and tuition I find that my higher nature must bear complete and easy sway over my lower nature; that the `old man' must be wholly put off and the `new man' wholly `put on'; that the affections and thoughts of my `inward man' must have easy and complete control over every appetite, passion, and desire of my `outward man'; and that I must keep myself so full of the Lord that I can live `a heavenly life upon earth", in all places and under all conceivable circumstances, just as easily and naturally as I can breathe the sweet air of heaven.

This loving and indescribable union with God is no longer a mere matter of faith with me, but it is a matter of actual knowledge and sweet experience... While enjoying these heavenly experiences the Lord has given me better health than during any eleven months for the last twenty years. And He has dealt more tenderly with me than any human mother ever dealt with a helpless infant.

I sincerely hope that the love and goodness of the Lord, so bountifully manifested in giving such large foretastes of heaven while yet in the body, will prove helpful and encouraging to every honest-hearted reader. But since the ways of the Lord are infinite in variety, let no one look for an experience precisely like mine. I have prayed for years that the Lord would make me just as pure, just as holy and just as useful as lay within the scope of human and Divine possibilities. He is now taking His own way to answer my prayers."

— "Under the Divine Touch", by Chester E. Pond, No. 1432 Chestnut St., Philadelphia, Pa. First published in the Mount Joy "Herald", Mt. Joy, Pa., under dates of April 8 and 15, 1882.

In the following experience, it will be seen that this so-called Divine touch reveals itself as that of a Borderland BRIDEGROOM. It is taken from a letter written by a lady, a devout and pure-minded Christian, as will be noticed. Her experiences occurred at a well-known summer resort in the United States where a cottage for divine healing had been established. But as the letter was shown to me by a third party, I do not feel at liberty to mention the town, lest some clue be given to the writer's personality. Indeed, it was only on this condition that the person who showed me this letter allowed me to make use of it herewith.

"Dear Sister N...—Since learning from Miss X. that you know the experience which is mine, I have thought I should write to you.

At first, as the newly married BRIDE, I shrank from exposing the secrets of my "Love". They were sacred between my Beloved and myself. Now, it has shown me that this wondrous truth, as well as all other truth, must be acknowledged, and that a most glorious part of my high calling is to cooperate with Him in calling His BRIDE unto Himself.

For myself, I had not time to question; the truth was sprung upon me unexpectedly, and I just went under. The fears and questionings came afterwards; but blessed be my God! He did not let me parley long with the foe, but Himself strengthened me to shake off his power and, coming fully under the shelter of *His love*, press on—until He had fully established me, and I, impelled by His might Spirit within me, reach eagerly forward to the glorious unfolding of *His love* and *power* that lie beyond.

"Suffice it to say, I am in great and abundant fullness and blessing, alike in my physical and in my spiritual nature, and that His own abounding life flows *in power* through my *whole being*.

I would have it *fully understood* that this is the fulfilment of the marriage relation between *Christ and the body*—that as he has been recognized in the soul as Lord over it, and also over the other parts and organs of the body, so now must He be recognized and accepted in the organs of generation as Lord over them; and *His life* must be allowed to come in, where, through fear of evil, the motions of life have heretofore been suppressed. Satan is bound to beset the soul with fears, it may be the most terrible, and to whisper, perhaps, dreadful things. The only way is to remember the faithfulness of Him who has led us these many years—*never* betraying our *confidence*. Standing upon the written word, and casting ourselves in complete abandonment upon Him, let Him have His way in every part. The life abundant must flow into every part of His *purchased possession* ere we are *fully* redeemed.

Inasmuch as we withhold from Him one part or organ, we are robbing God of just this much. God has given us no idle words in his written Word; EVERY PROMISE is to be realized by us, as we follow on, and enter into the experience portrayed in each particular position of the word.

"'The Body, the Temple of God'. I. Thess. IV. 3, 4; I. Cor. III. 16-19.

"'The Living Sacrifice'. Rom. VI. II. 12, 13; VIII. 10-13; Rom. XII. 1.

"'The BRIDE and Husband'. Isaiah XXVI. 9; LIV. 5; Cant. III. 1; Eph. V. 29-32; 22, 23; 2Cor. XI. 2; I. Cor. XII. 21-23; Col. I. 25-27; Ezek. XXVI. 25; Hos. II. 14-16; John XVII. 23; Hos. XIX. 20; Hos. VI. 3; Rev. XIX. 7-9; Rev. ch. XXI; Ezek. ch XIII, to end.

"The Song of Solomon was not to be a dead letter, but meant by the Holy Ghost to be the experience of the *BRIDE of Christ* I find God now in wondrous reality in His written Word. The meaning, hitherto unknown, of different passages, stands out clear and distinct—and the Living Word within me, throbbing and thrilling and permeating my whole being with His glorious Presence, bears witness of the written truth.

One day, I read in the Word, being led to it, the assurance of the angel concerning Mary. Perhaps that day—or very soon after—the Spirit brought to me, as I was preparing dinner—'Fear not, that which is conceived

within thee is of the Holy Spirit'. Such a
rapid and powerful witness to the Word went
through and through me, beginning at the
organs of generation, going all through, what
I was in great weakness, physically. The
tempter had been busy about this time, casting fear upon me lest the flesh were in the
matter. Thus the Spirit gave him answer—
with the revelation came the thought, `I am
with child!' —but so sure was the witness,
that instead of being greatly alarmed—
*praise* the Blessed One, a great joy welled
up within me at the thought of such a possibility. A *glorious victory*, afterwards. He
showed me that it meant that this precious
truth of the marriage relation between us
was, `that which was in me was of the Holy
Ghost.' *Praise the Lord!* He has made me
willing to do—to bear—to suffer anything for
Him. He is making me fearless and filling
me with His own desire for the spread of
*all* his *truth*—though I feel more especially the desire to win souls for Him. I am
assured that this, His most glorious and sat-
isfying revelation of Himself, *must* be
acknowledged as He shall call upon us to do
so, or we shall come into darkness indeed,
and distress. Shall the chosen and honored
wife shame to confess her husband when he
would *woo* others, through her, to the same
high place?

When we enter into this union He is, as
never before, the Life within us, and how
shall we seek to suppress the Life that has
entered in to displace our own old self-life,
and to manifest Himself in and through us,

in *whatever way He wills*. He must be permitted to speak through us—and as I constantly pray, to *love, through me*. Oh! with us there must be no question but one, viz.: `What wilt Thou, my Beloved?'—and ready response, opening up to meet His blessed will.

*`As Thou wilt'—no longer I, but *Christ*'. No more *my* will, in the slightest particular, but the adorable will of my Beloved.

Reading Madam Guyon in `Spiritual Progress', Part II, on `Union with God', I find the experience into which I have entered.

We have, in these last days, by the [words missing] been realizing, as we did in the earlier days, the Presence and power of Him whom we *love*. God comes upon us as we meet together from 6 to 7 o'clock in the morning, to wait in silence before Him—at the table, before and after meals; as we partake of the food He gives. We meet Him in our rooms, and bow down before Him. As I go about my work, ofttimes, His Presence so fills me—or I hear the sweet wooing of His voice, until I am constrained to step aside, where I may—to be *alone* with my *Love*, and fall at His feet in adoring worship.

One asks, how is this Baptism obtained? In the *same way* exactly that all other of His gifts are—if we are in the condition to receive them, that is, by faith. He says, `Thy Maker is thy husband', and `in that day thou shalt call me—Ishi'.

I would say, whatever you do, do not question, lest distress and perplexity come in; but immediately go to Jesus, accepting Him as Ishi—with the words I have given—`be it unto me as Thou wilt'. He will do the teaching afterwards. Then, again, lest one should make of it too scriptural a truth, separating it entirely from the physical, it should be plainly understood that the *union* is as the sexual intercourse of husband and wife.

If we expect this, when the sensation comes we will not be alarmed, but willingly and freely give those parts to our Divine Husband as the *BRIDE* would naturally do.

I have written very plainly because, first, I *know* it is the way *He* would have me write; and secondly, because I would seek to save from distress and fear, that would harass, if the whole truth is not understood, viz.: If one looks for one kind of manifestation (spiritual), and finds physical and animal.

Let me hear from you both, when the Lord leads.

"Lovingly, in Him, ......."

The same friend who showed me the above letter also showed me letters from a gentleman who is the editor of a religious newspaper, giving a similar experience, upon several occasions in his life but with more circumstance of detail. Nevertheless, he regarded it as entirely a union with Christ, the BRIDEGROOM of the Soul, and spoke of it reverently.

Madam de Guyon has left us memoirs of her rapturous union with the Divine BRIDEGROOM of the Soul, and verses concerning His love and watchful tenderness which are rare specimens of pure and delicate sentiment. Yet, so little was Borderland wedlock understood by the learned of those days, that Bossuet made a coarse joke about her marriage with the Child Jesus; and another French bishop says Arthur Little wrote what might almost be called an episcopal lampoon. One couplet will be enough:

*"Par l'epoux quelque foi une jeune mystique
Entend un autre epoux que celui du cantique."*

("A young woman who is mystical understand another spouse than that of Canticles.") From which it would seem as though the Roman Catholic Church admits that there might be objective realities in Borderland wedlock (so far at least as appears on the surface), and eschews objective phenomena on the Borderland and tries to keep her mystics entirely in the realm of subjectivity— a realm where illusions arise through the ease with which it is confounded with objective planes, and where a well-trained mind is needed to distinguish between that which is suggested or thought hypnotically and that which actually occurs. And yet, it is for a Divine BRIDEGROOM on the Borderland that the Church has long trained her nuns in the life of ascetics. For in various forms of austere self-denial, asceticism as well as total suppression of the sex-nature is an absolute preliminary step to Borderland nuptials, though only for a time.

The question arises, however: who is this Divine Spouse of the purified and ecstatic nun? Is it Christ? Or is it an angelic lover? The Church says Christ, when the union is uplifting and insists that the relation is entirely mystical and not at all objective.

I think from the testimonies which I have adduced from church writings that an angelic BRIDEGROOM is not impossible. And it is quite conceivable that, where a nun believes that Christ is the only Borderland Spouse, her prejudice may result in her lover appearing to her as Christ, just as the mediaeval witch who believed that her Borderland spouse could only be the Devil was pretty sure to see him with horns and hooves and to be whisked away (subjectively) to a Witch's Sabbath of diablerie.

Madam de Guyon, indeed, admits that "the vision is never of God himself nor scarcely ever of Jesus Christ, as those who have it picture it to themselves; it is an Angel of Light, who according to the power which is given to him by God for this purpose causes the soul to see his representation, which it takes for himself." (That is, the vision is subjective, probably an hypnotic suggestion induced by the angel.)

The following stories of saintly Catholic women who became espoused to a Borderland **BRIDEGROOM** show that they were untrained in distinguishing subjective from objective phenomena. No wonder, then, if they should mistake an angel for Christ himself.

*St. Mary Magdalene, born of the illustrious house of the Pazzi at Florence, burned with so great a heat of divine love that she would at times exclaim "O love, I can bear thee no longer!", and she used to be forced to cool her bosom with a copious sprinkling of water.*

*By Christ she was wedded with a ring, and crowned with a crown of thorns; whilst by the Blessed Virgin she was covered with a most white veil, and by St. Augustine she had twice written upon her heart, "the Word as made flesh". Being rapt out of her sense while embroidering she used, though the windows were closed up and her eyes veiled, to proceed with her work and finish it most accurately. She was canonized by Clement IX in 1669.*

— Breviary — Nuns and Nunneries, 37-

St. Rose of Lima:

"*The first flower of sanctity from America was the Virgin Rose, born of Christian parents at Lima, who even from the cradle shone with the presages of future holiness; for the face of the infant being wonderfully transfigured into the image of a rose, gave occasion to her being called by this name to which afterwards the Virgin Mother of God added the surname, ordering her to be henceforth called the Rose of Mary. At the age of five she made a vow of perpetual virginity.*

"*Having wondrously familiar intercourse, by continual apparitions, with her guardian angel, with St. Catharine of Sienna, and the Virgin Mother of God she merited to hear these words from Christ—Rose of my heart, be thou my spouse. At last being carried to the Paradise of this her spouse and glittering with very many miracles, both before and since her departure. Pope Clement X enrolled her with solemnity in the Catalogue for Holy Virgins.*"

The following are extracts from the Bull of her canonization:

"*At this time she was favoured with the following revelation: There appeared to her in her sleep an extraordinary person, beautiful above all the sons of men habited like a sculptor on a festival-day, and he seemed to court her as a lover. Before Rose would consent to his proposal she set him a task, namely, to carve a piece of marble; and she bade him return again shortly, when the sculpture would be finished. At the return of her spouse the virgin blushed when she perceived the task she had*

*assigned him was accomplished in a manner be-
yond his strength and he opened to her his
workshop where was a number of elect virgins,
working like men at carving and polishing marble.*

*She discovered that they were his espoused, by
the style and beauty of their nuptial dresses; they
were moistening the stones, and preparing them for
cutting by their tears, which dripped upon them.
Rose perceived that she was to be dressed like one
of them, and prepared to be advanced to a like espousal.[words missing] The mystery was disclosed to
her thus:*

*On Palm Sunday, when Rose was absorbed in
meditation, in the chapel of the Blessed Virgin of
the Rosary, her lover thus addressed her: `Rose of
my heart, be my love'. The virgin trembled at the
sweet voice of her Divine Spouse and at the instant
she heard the voice of the Mother of God wishing
her joy, and saying, `Rose, it is no mean honour
which this my Son proposes to you.'*

*After this revelation, Rose began to torture her-
self more than ever. When her Spouse did not
appear to her at the accustomed hour, she used to
admit an angel (who was always visibly present with
her as her guardian) to her confidence, as his foot-
boy or valet (ut pararium aut veredareum)."*

Various miracles were said to have been
wrought through St. Rose of Lima: such as,
for instance, the materialization of bread and
also of honey in her father's house in time of
scarcity also, in answer to prayer, the pay-
ment of a debt of her father by a stranger who

appeared at the house, bringing the money wrapped up in a cloth.

> *"These are the assistance's which her divine Spouse promised to the parents of Rose, that he would give her as a dowry, when he wooed her in the character of a heavenly sculptor."*

In this last, we seem to be getting back to these angelic BRIDEGROOMS spoken of in ante-Nicene Christian literature, who materialized gold and other precious articles for beloved earthly spouses.

But, it may be asked, are these unions with a heavenly spouse mere marital unions with angels, and does God (or Christ, as His human manifestation) play the part in them? By no means. God is a party to Borderland wedlock in its highest aspect, whether that wedlock be an objective marriage union (as in earthly wedlock) or a subjective and mystical blending with a divine invisible intelligence. Mme. de Guyon was right in saying that her love toward God and God's love toward her was the blissful feature in Borderland experience. There are lower aspects of Borderland wedlock than that which includes union with God; which are subject more or less to illusions, fantastical or diabolical. Only when the earthly partner aspires to the Divine Soul of all things does the supreme bliss of union with the angelic mate transpire. At such times one is fain to apply such a conception as that of Mrs. Gillen, a London teacher of Divine Healing, which is:

*"The Universe consists of three factors: a Thinker, the outward Expression of His thought, and the realm of Mentality which lies between that Thinker and His Expression, and which is the means by which the Uncreate shapes what it thinks into Expression in physical, material forms. If we conceive this Great Thinker (God) as the central nucleus of a great circle (This should be, of course, a sphere, and it is thus that Mrs. Gillen prefers to conceive the Universe. But a circle, being flat, is easier of comprehension by non-mathematicians when divided into sectors, and I have therefore adopted Mrs. Gillen's method of this easier representation.), which embraces the Universe, his Expression of thoughts, motives, feelings, will be on the rim of the large circle, and the sphere of Mentality, where those thoughts are being moulded into shape previous to Expression, will be the zone lying between the nucleus, or Central Thinker, and the outer rim of His all-embracing circle. Each living creature, as part of this great circle, is a sector in the circle, thus:*

*Such a sector consists, as does the entire circle, likewise of three factors,*

*1. That which thinks;*

*2. Mentality, where thoughts are shaped;*

*3 The body, the material life, where spirit finds expression as outward form."*

Nos. 2 and 3—mentality and the bodily form—are but the instruments of the spirit, the thinker within us. The thinker within us is part of the Great Thinker at the centre of the circle of the Universe. So that, according to Mrs. Gillen, it is incorrect to say "I *have* spirit." We should say "I *am* a spirit", i.e., "I am a part of God". When the zone of our mentality is kept unclouded between our material, bodily form and that within us up at the point of the sector which thinks, we are, as will be seen, in unbroken communication with the Great Thinker, God, who is Himself all in all: for our thinking self is part of Him. The application of this conception, from Mrs. Gillen's point of view, is that when that zone of mentality is un-clouded by dislike or other antitheses of love, then disease and other mundane annoyances no longer exist for us; since, being part of God, and being one with Him at the heart of the Universe, we have His power to create outward circumstances.

From my own point of view, this concep-tion has a bearing on the third and highest degree in the mysteries of Borderland wedlock. But before enlarging this, it may be well to begin with the preliminary training necessary to render one the Borderland wife or husband of an angel and to set forth the three degrees in order with such detail as may be allowable in a work like this, which is in-tended for the general public. The readers hope to profit by these instructions for personal development, inasmuch as if one can persuade one's earthly partner to try, with one's self, to live the life which is obligatory for Borderland wedlock, it brings the Kingdom of heaven into earthly relations.

The preliminary training necessary may be summed up by the admonition: Live a correct moral life, according to our own highest standard (a standard, by the way, which should never be fixed, but always moving onward to still greater excellence), and strive to think clearly and to form accurate conceptions of ideas, to express conceptions with exactness, and to follow Truth, wherever she leads, and whatever your previous convictions upon any given subject. Especially, you must have such high and clean thoughts about sex that you can think about it, read about it, and talk about all the details without agitation, without grossness of thought, and with as impersonal a state of mind as if you were discussing the circulation of the blood. And you must learn to recognize the educational value of sex attraction in the evolution of humanity from savagery into civilization. Chiefest of all, learn that sex is holy before God and the angels. During this preliminary training, all sex union must be refrained from absolutely. The nervous energy which has hitherto been evoked for expenditure in this direction must no longer be expended, but, by continual self-mastery, be returned to the system for its upbuilding. Gradually, as the neophyte who has habituated himself to a pure-minded and idealistic conception of sex becomes accustomed to thus maintaining self-poise, no matter what the temptation, there will spring up in him a joy in his own power which will amply repay him for all his struggles.

The first degree embodies the teaching of what is known as Alpha-ism. Its principle is:

"No sex union except for the distinct purpose of begetting a child".

The bearings of this principle will be discussed in my forthcoming treatise on "Psychic Wedlock". Suffice it to say here that the staunch adherence to this principle has uplifted and brightened the lives of many husbands and wives who had begun to find the marriage state a hell on earth. But it is a mistake to consider this the most advanced teaching regarding the marital relation. It is beautiful, helpful, and necessary to acquire for those who would live the life of the truly wedded; but it is only the first of the three steps which lead husband and wife up to the ideal relations. In "The Christian Life", a journal edited and published by Rev. J.D. Caldwell, Chicago, the teaching of Alpha-ism will be found set forth clearly and reverently.

Following this should come another pamphlet called "Diana", written by Prof.

Parkhurst, the astronomer, and published by the Burnz Publishing Co., New York. This pamphlet is, unfortunately, marred by being printed in the reform spelling, but one forgets after a page or two. It is a psycho-physiological essay, intended for husbands and wives; written from a high standpoint, and in refined language. "Diana" will furnish the initiate with a bridge between the first and second degrees; and it is one of the most important and helpful contributions to the sex question that have ever been published.

It is evident that this first degree is likely to prove a stumbling block to those who degrade this beautiful principle of Alpha-ism (a principle embodied in the Scriptural command, "Be fruitful and multiply") into an excuse for sowing more seed than is needed to produce the harvest.

The man or woman who, whether on Borderland or in earthly wedlock, thus persistently distorts the above Scriptural command into a permission for something very different from what was intended will never get beyond the first degree of the marriage relation. To create children is not only a high and holy joy to every right-thinking husband and wife, it is a solemn duty imposed upon them by the laws of their own being. And the psychic who shirks this duty in Borderland wedlock, although maintaining marital relations by the angelic spouse, will be misled by all sorts of fantastic or diabolical illusions. Conversely, wedded on the Borderland to an angel, holds fast the thought of the duty of the married to create (*under suitable conditions*), will ere long be shown the truth, i.e., that between two people dwelling on entirely different planes of matter, while the marital relation is possible, lawful and beautiful, to beget a child is impossible until the earthly partner shall have crossed to the world beyond the grave.

The principle of Alpha-ism must be mastered by those who aspire to the second degree, whether on the Borderland or on the Earthly plane. The second and the third degrees have this principle for their cornerstone. In none of the three degrees is it allowable to sow the seed except for the distinct purpose of begetting a child who has been reverently and prudently planned for at just that time. Nor is it ever allowable to waste the seed by throwing it away (and with it the psychic energy). The second degree launches the initiate upon the perilous waters of sense-gratification. If his previous training has enabled him to build a staunch craft for the voyage, well and good; otherwise, he may be swamped at the first wave, or, if he rides its crest, and the crests of succeeding waves, he may rashly venture too near the fatal rapids and be engulfed. It is possible that was the error into which Josephus says the "giants" fell when they trusted in their own strength. The second degree was practiced in the Oneida Community for thirty years, and was obligatory upon all its male members. The result was highly satisfactory, despite the society's unsavory practice of community of women. They do not seem, however, to have seen the necessity for a similar training of female members.

The author of that popular novel, "The Strike of a Sex", has been preparing a book called "Zugassent's Theory", which is intended to deal with this method from a popular standpoint. I have not seen the work (which I believe is now going through the press); but from what I know of the author's reputation and his efforts hitherto in the cause of social purity, I feel that the book is likely to be judiciously worded and to be an aid in mastering the second degree. I doubt, however, if it deals with the training of the feminine partner. But the principles underlying the training of the man may be studied out from such a work and applied by the woman. The author is George N. Miller, 59 Murray St., N.Y. The second degree is the most difficult of the three degrees to acquire, physiologically speaking, inasmuch as it exacts supreme self-control at a crucial moment. Those who have never attempted this degree, when told of it, are apt to either declare it impossible, or to scorn it as undesirable.

But those who have once mastered this degree would no more forego the power which is now theirs than a freed prisoner would voluntarily return to his dungeon. This way lies the path of liberty and life and joy, and they who have once trodden it in the perfect fulness of magnetic union with a dearly loved spouse will never care to stumble along the old paths. The Oneida Community, despite its social mistake of promiscuity has made the human race its everlasting debtor, in that it has left a thirty years' scientific experiment on record detailing the methods and attesting the value of this second degree.

But let it never be forgotten that this second degree must be built upon the first degree, Alpha-ism. To make use of it as a means to increased sensuality is to degrade it, and to do so effectually bars the initiate from entrance upon that third and highest degree where all joys, physical, mental, emotional and spiritual, reach an intensity besides which the joys of the first and second degrees pale as a candle-flame pales in the radiance of sunlight. Moreover, if this degree be thus degraded by the initiate, it is almost certain to bring nervous diseases of a very distressing character in its train.

On the third, and highest degree, no book has yet been written, so far as I know. The teaching seems to have been handed down orally, or else by pictured symbolism or mystic rite, understood only by the initiates of this degree. I am now compiling notes for my work on "Psychic Wedlock" which I hope will take up the projected three degrees in more detail than is possible in this treatise. For the present, I can only lay down a few general principles, and these principles which cannot be fully grasped by any except those who have mastered the first and second degrees.

The Hindus have the theory that God can enjoy food, drink, and, in fact, all sense-pleasures only through the offering of an earthly devotee. Therefore, the devout Hindu offers God a share in all his gratifications of appetite—thus living out, indeed, the Christian Apostle's admonition of "whether we eat or drink, do all to the glory of God". Too often, it is true, this doctrine is perverted into an excuse for sensual excesses, the debauchee soothing his conscience by an offering to the god whom he worships. Thus has this sacred inner mystery become degraded by the unworthy, even by the tried and staunch initiate of the first and second degree, unless he holds grace as he enters upon this third degree, unless he holds fast to the teaching, "aspire to the highest". Only in reverent and earnest aspiration to the Divine, to the source of all things, to the Eternal Energy of the Universe, may this third degree be entered upon, either in Borderland or in earthly wedlock. The more intense the emotion, the more absolute the necessity for aspiring with all one's faculties to union with the Divine. Every element of selfish desire must be eliminated; one must aspire at that time because it is right and beautiful to bring one's holiest and tenderest and most ecstatic emotions into the presence of the Great Thinker, in order that they may there be purged of all dross and be a worthy expression of our own best self.

That is the first half of this highest degree. The second half is entered upon when spontaneously—not from selfish desire—it dawns upon us that to offer God a share of our pleasure at that moment may give Him pleasure. When single-heartedly and in all sincerity and benevolent feeling toward God we invite him to become the third partner in the marital union, then, indeed, do we understand what it is to love and be loved. We enter thus into a personal relation with God, in which, Impersonal Force though He be we realize vividly that we are one with Him, and with Him one with all the universe. For that in us which thinks—the apex of our particular sector of the circle of the universe—is, on the one hand, in unclouded relation with our physical self on the outer rim, and on the other hand, it is merged into the Great Thinker, the Great Nucleus who is at the centre of all creation.

From that moment, we are able to say to this Pantheos, Great Thinker, to this All-Pervading Energy, "My *friend*!" (And inasmuch as God is love in the fullest possible sense of that expression, the connubial bliss of Borderland lovers is increased tenfold). From that moment, we know what it is truly to love God. This divine trinity in unity must be the final goal of Borderland wedlock, if such wedlock is to be permanent.

It is in this sense, I am inclined to think, that Mme. de Guyon, St. Teresa, and other mystical Spouses of Christ, received the Divine BRIDEGROOM. Subjectively mingled with this rapturous union with Deity, no doubt, were the experiences of union with the angelic husband, of whose very existence as such they were unaware, confounding him with the Impersonal Deity who was the third element in their union. Then, too, we must remember that these women, intelligent as they were, were untrained in the nice distinctions of the subjective and the objective, hallucinatory, veridical, automatic, telepathic, subconscious, etc., evolved by the modern Society for Psychical Research and other recent investigators of the occult.

Moreover, there are psychical experiences in Borderland wedlock which are subjective while they seem to the untrained occultist to be objective. Of such a nature (apparently) was the experience of a Philadelphia lady, a Spiritualist, who told me of her spirit husband. She was a widow, and this spirit was a deceased lover from whom she had been separated in youth by a misunderstanding. He returned from the world beyond the grave to explain matters, and to reclaim his lost love, and finally proposed that she should consider herself to be his wife from that time on, assuring her that it was so recorded in his land. Thereafter, on several occasions, she experienced (when she was by no means prepared) a series of galvanic shocks extending upwards through her body. These were doubtless hypnotic suggestions to prepare and train her for experiences of a more objective character. The manifestations, however, were interfered with by the return of a chronic complaint of the liver with which she had suffered at intervals for years.

If it be asked how a misty, vaporous being, such as a ghost is popularly supposed to be, can sustain an objective marital union on the Borderland, I reply that the ghost is not mistlike in reality, but only appears so because he is in a new world of matter, with a more extended scale of vibrations per second for the various forces of sound, heat, light, and electricity than obtain upon our earthly plane.

Beyond the last faint violet ray of the spectrum, science has demonstrated that there are rays of color to which we are blind, but which so lowly a creature as the ant can perceive. Dogs can trace a scent of which we have no perception. Many people are so color-blind as to be unable to distinguish a red from a green light—a fact brought out some years since very markedly in an examination for railways service in England. An astigmatic person is almost, if not quite, blind to a fine line running in some one direction. Recent experiments by Galton have shown that cats and birds are sensitive to a whistle which is inaudible to the human ear. If our inferiors in the animal Kingdom reveal such marked superiority to ourselves in sensitiveness to vibrations, is it unlikely that our former equal, now our superior, the deceased human being who has passed out of earth-life into a wider realm, shall also acquire sensitiveness to a wider range of vibrations? The ghost probably senses all things on our plane, plus a great many more things on his own. Our sensations are included in his, but his extend far on each side of our own. Therefore we cannot perceive his form or hear his voice in all his material relations, because he is in a world where forms, colors, sounds which we are physically incapable of perceiving—except in the exalted condition of the Clairvoyant or Clairaudient—are part and parcel of his daily life. When we see him, we see only through the narrow range of our own limited scale of vibrations; so that we see him but in part, and therefore mistily, or hear his voice but faintly, or perhaps not at all, as it may cover a range of vibrations per second quite one side or the other of our own scale of sound vibrations.

For this reason, he is often obliged to speak to the psychic by the interior voice—an hypnotic rendition, apparently, of his voice through the medium of her subconsciousness. For this reason, because his voice is not audible, as a rule, to her physical ears, the psychic must learn to discriminate accurately between this interior voice and the voiced imaginings of her own sub-consciousness, which will utter themselves quite as audibly as does the interior voice if the psychic has not acquired the faculty of holding her sub-consciousness well under control. With experience, however, the discrimination comes in time to be made unerringly, as St. Teresa has stated.

Through the interior voice, a Borderland mystic may be wooed and won as a wife if she be clear-headed and keep the moral law with scrupulous care. She does not need to be clairaudient to hear her lover's voice interiorly. Nor does she need to be clairvoyant if she be willing to go it blindly, so to say. She is then in the condition, however, of a person who is totally blind; and who is almost totally deaf. Since she needs to be on the alert quite as much as if she were dependent on an ear-trumpet, in order to make no mistake in catching the remarks made by the interior voice. Nevertheless, even people who are blind and people who are deaf may fall in love with someone on this earthly plane and marry despite the defective means of communicating ideas. Fortunately there are other means of transmitting ideas than by the interior voice or by the eye or the ear. In this connection the following article by Paul Tyner, on "The Sixth Sense and How to Develop It" in "The Arena" offers a suggestive thought.

"I have said that I regard psychometry as the key to the development, on rational lines, of the sixth sense. Psychometry itself seems to be a development on the psychic side of that physical sense, which is at once the finest, the most subtle, the most comprehensive, and the most neglected of all the five senses—the sense of *touch*. While distributed over the whole surface of the body, through the nervous system, this sense is more delicate and sensitive in some parts than in others. The marvelous possibilities of its development in the hands are shown in the cases of expert silk buyers and of coin handlers. The first are enabled merely by touch to distinguish instantly the weight and fineness of a score of different pieces of cloth hardly distinguishable to the eye. Girls employed in the mints, while counting gold and silver coins at an astonishingly rapid speed, detect at once the minutest difference of overweight or underweight in the coin passing through their hands. The remarkable sensitiveness developed by the blind in the tips of the fingers, under such scientific cultivation as that provided in the Perkins Institute, of which Laura Bridgman in the past and Helen Keller in the present, are such conspicuous examples, is familiar to most readers.

It may not be so generally known that recent postmortem examinations of the bodies of the blind reveal the fact that in the nerves at the ends of the fingers, well-defined cells of gray matter had formed, identical *in substance and in cell formation with the grey matter of the brain. What does this show? If brain and nerves are practically identical, is it not plain that, instead of being confined to the cavity of the skull, there is not any part of the surface of the body that can be touched by a pin's point without pricking the brain? It shows, moreover, I think, that all the sensations generally received through the other physical organs of sense may be received through the touch at the tips of the fingers. It proves that a man can think not alone in his head, but all over his body, and especially in the great nerve centers like the "solar plexus", and the nerve ends, on the palms of the hands and the soles of the feet. The coming man will assuredly perceive and think in every part, from his head down to his feet. Need I suggest the importance of remembering, in this connection, how much in our modern life is conveyed by the hand clasp, of the deep delight that comes to lovers in caressing touches, when impelled to pat the hands or cheek of the beloved one, or to stroke her hair? It is through the emotional life that our sensitiveness is led from the physical to the psychic plane of sensation."*

It is through the nerves of touch that Borderland wedlock becomes objective. The lover may remain forever invisible, as in the fairy stories, materializing only at night, and then only to the touch of those nerves most capable of sensing this tangibility. But, ghost though he may be, it was the testimony of Reginald Scott in his "Discoverie of Witchcraft" that the Witch "hath more pleasure that way, they say, than with anie mortall man."

The angelic BRIDEGROOM, as well as his earthly partner, must live a correct moral life and think clearly; and this means that he must exercise a tenderness, a considerate regard for his wife's comfort and happiness, and also a marital self-control of which too many earthly men are ignorant. No wonder, then, that on the plane of sentiment she should prefer this ghostly spouse to "anie mortall man". And on the plane of physiological relations, I think I have already shown that the husband who is an initiate in the third degree, who has trained his wife therein, can assure her of "connubial bliss which is perpetual". The Borderland BRIDEGROOM has this advantage, too, over the earthly BRIDEGROOM: being able to read his partner's thoughts, he can adapt himself to her most delicate fluctuations of sentiment at a moment's warning, and so never fail to be truly her companion.

"If one could prolong the happiness of love into marriage", wrote Rousseau, "we should have Paradise on earth".

In my own case, Paradise—the Kingdom of Heaven—has come into my earth life. And it has come through my HEAVENLY BRIDEGROOM.

— THE END —

# Jabberwoke Pocket Occult Collection

### CRYSTAL GAZING by Frater Achad

Thus, it is hoped, all will be satisfied; and should their satisfaction be equal to that of the Author at this opportunity to herald the Light – however faintly – of the Ultimate Crystalline Sphere.

ISBN: 978-1-954873-36-0
$ 11.00 USD
FraterAchadCrystalGazing.com

### HEAVENLY BRIDEGROOMS by Ida Craddock

"One of the most remarkable human documents ever produced... This book is of incalculable value to every student of Occult matters. No Magick library is complete without it" – A.C.

ISBN: 978-1-954873-21-6
$ 14.00 USD
HeavenlyBridegrooms.com

### MOONCHILD by Aleister Crowley

The cattiest & messiest novel from the transcriber of the Wickedest Man in England. Hiding behind the guise of fiction, Moonchild is the Beast's platform to slander his many nemeses inside the spiritualist circles of London.

ISBN: 978-1-954873-53-7
$ 19.00 USD /
AleisterCrowleyMoonchild.com

### THE KYBALION by Three Initiates

There is no portion of the occult teachings which has been so closely guarded as the fragments of the Hermetic Teachings, the Great Central Sun of Occultism, whose rays have illuminated the teachings promulgated since time.

ISBN: 978-1-954873-08-7
$ 14.00 USD
ThreeInitiatesKybalion.com

### THE SO-CALLED OCCULT by Carl Jung

A 20-year-old Carl Jung attends his cousin's seance, leading to a psychological investigation of hauntings, witch-sleeps, and delicious bliss that unravels in obsession.

ISBN: 978-1-954873-39-1
$ 14.00 USD
TheSoCalledOccult.com

### THE GREAT GOD PAN *by Arthur Machen*

A classic of pagan horror that follows the trail of destruction left in the wake of a mysterious socialite, as she serves the will of her shadowy, horned benefactor.

ISBN: 978-1-954873-35-3
$14.00 USD
AllHailPan.com

### THE WITCH CULT *by Margaret Murray*

Firsthand accounts of a pre-Christian witch cult that worshiped the Horned God of fertility—whose Christian persecutors referred to him as the Devil—and the nocturnal rites performed at the witches' Sabbath.

ISBN: 978-1-954873-33-9
$19.00 USD
TheWitchCult.com

### THE BOOK OF LIES *by Frater Perdurabo*

A collection of falsehoods from Dionysus, received by the mysterious Frater Perdurabo and the Scarlet Woman LAYLAH. This wicked book is said to contain within its pages the secret truth of the universe . . . readers beware.

ISBN: 978-1-954873-37-7
$14.00 USD
FaleslyCalledBreaks.com

### A MIDSOMMAR NIGHT'S DREAM *by William Shakespeare*

The timeless ethereal tale of four Lovers who wander too close to the games of Titania and Oberon, the Faerie Queen and King, and their encounters with the archetypal Tickster Puck and all the fantastical beings whom inhabit the woodland realm.

ISBN: 978-1-954873-54-4
$11.00 USD
MidsommarNightsDream.com

### SATAN: A NOVEL *by Mark Twain*

The greatest and final novel from the master of American fiction, Mark Twain's fable of an angelic visitation in the Austrian countryside reveals the solipsism of its author, and his belief of the unreality of our collective dream.

ISBN: 978-1-954873-59-9
$16.00 USD
MarkTwainSatan.com

CPSIA information can be obtained
at www.ICGtesting.com
Printed in the USA
FSHW010011280921
85000FS